All my
EGGS
in one
BASKET

FRANCINE RAYMOND
Photographs by Sarah Bush

The KITCHEN GARDEN

Published in Great Britain by
The Kitchen Garden 2007
www.kitchen-garden-hens.co.uk
01359 268 322

ISBN 978-0-9532857-9-2

Other Books from the Kitchen Garden:
Keeping a Few Hens in Your Garden
More Hens in the Garden
Food from the Kitchen Garden
Beekeeping for Beginners
Keeping a few Ducks in Your Garden
Peacock on the Lawn
Goose on the Green

Henkeeper's Journal
Christmas Journal
The Big Book of Garden Hens

With many thanks to Sarah for her breathtaking photographs, to Max for his
patient computer expertise, to Jackie Bennett for her editor's overview, to Penny,
Rena, Carol and Barbara who donated recipes, Susie Carrington for her eagle
eye, and to all those I abandoned whilst concentrating on this book.

"Francine Raymond brings her qualities of affection, humour and practicality to this enchanting account of a year at the Kitchen Garden. As with her inimitable hen books, the tone here is encouraging, cheerful and tolerant; she has a peculiar gift for making the everyday activities of living into an art, and in reading her I find I learn as many hints for a happy and more serene home life as I do for garden and animal husbandry"

Raffaella Barker – Writer & Poultry Keeper

Welcome to the Kitchen Garden.

Join me, through the pages of this journal, in a year long wander through our high spots and low moments, via our milestones and markers, sampling the fruits of our labour, and meeting those, both fair and fowl, who shared life here during 2006.

Throughout life's inconsistencies, the garden provides constancy. And even though weather patterns nowadays are less predictable, seasonality isn't just based on the temperature or what's growing, but on celebrations, festivals and anniversaries, those jolly punctuations in life's bland script, those special thrills that familiarity never gets the chance to dull.

We'll all probably have to start finding our pleasures locally soon, so where better to begin than our own backyards? Befriend your inner hunter-gatherer. Even a small nod in the right direction helps: squeeze in a salad bed and forgo those chlorine-soaked packs; grow a few herbs in pots and wave goodbye to plants that flop on your window sill; or offer a roost to a couple of bantams and taste a truly fresh egg. Maybe rent an allotment, or share a garden, or perhaps just dream.

At the very least, shop seasonally and eat produce that involves less packaging, fewer food miles and more money in the right pockets, by patronising producers' markets and farm-gate shops. I'm as familiar as most with the shelves in my local supermarket, though I try to be discerning. Better companies sell locally sourced produce, and if you buy in season, there's always a choice.

3½ million of us work from home. How many more are housebound looking after children or relations, are retired or just idle rich? We can all enrich our lives, improving our health as we adapt our living space from pig's ear to silk purse, working with nature to avoid disease, and managing without fertilizers to feed our plants and pesticides to control predators. An organic garden doesn't have to look like a municipal tip covered in ancient carpet or stacked with car tyres, and well-managed hens won't wreck your plot.

I applaud anyone who cooks nowadays. Everything is stacked against us: the accepted ethos of fast food, our children's divergent tastes (how did that happen?) the availability of ready meals, and even M & S's television ads.

Cook a meal from scratch and you deserve a massive pat on the back, but good food has as much to do with sourcing and shopping for ingredients as the work-surface labour of chopping and cooking.

Life's pleasures are built up of simple transient moments, involving small rituals: the cups of tea, a child's favourite meal, the evening drink, the invalid's pick-me-up, breakfast in bed, meals outdoors in the company of friends - all these are within our grasp and trump mass-produced highs.

To point you in the right direction, I'd like to share a year here with you, suggesting recipes, gardening tips and hen keeping hints en route, offering glimpses into life here at home. Home, as Mole in *Wind in the Willows* recognizes, is a special place, an anchorage in everyone's existence.

JANuary

1st

This is a cold house. Lovely in summer, when the interior and garden merge, just about bearable during spring and autumn, with the Rayburn taking the edge off the chill, but the minute the temperature drops to below zero and one isn't involved in energetic pursuits, it is cold.

Here I am, typing away with stiff fingers, in layer upon layer of clothes – some of which belie my early career as a fashion designer. An invaluable M & S knitted silk vest is overlaid with a cast-off Stussy T-shirt, a sheepskin waistcoat, and a thick jumper – vintage 1985. My feet are warm in outdoor boots, but I'm wearing a silk scarf, topped with my son's jaunty Carhartt woollen hat. My nose is red despite applications of Saint Laurent's Touche Eclat, because keeping the fires fed is a full time job. And today the kindling is damp.

In failing light, I drive to the next village and the local shop. Thank god, at least we have a shop nearby. A magnificent emporium that stocks everything you could ever need. I'm told the kindling is in one of the abandoned cars that owner's husband hasn't quite got round to repairing. Wading through an oil-laden puddle, I open the door to a seat full of dried pig's ears (doggy chews) and overwhelmed by the stench, grab a bundle of wood from the back seat and drive home. Even after 25 years, country living is still an eye-opener. Once lit though, the fire warms me and the house becomes a friend again.

2nd

The Old Cockerel died last night. He just gave up the ghost. Struggling manfully for the past few days to keep up with his ladies, he just stayed in the henhouse yesterday, and at bedtime, we found him dead. He was a good old boy, and at five years old, the lifespan of most Buff Orpington cocks, he succumbed to a heart attack.

3rd

Got up early to dig a huge hole to bury him, in one of the empty compost bays. He was so enormous, it took forever. All that magnificent fluff and feather, what a waste. I should have had him stuffed by that taxidermist with the shop on Islington Green. Then I could take him with me, on display, to talks and courses.

Now I need to decide which of two young cockerels to keep, the loser has a home waiting in Woodbridge. There is barely a feather in it. I've earmarked a likely candidate whose main appeal so far is his friendliness to me (hard to resist, but not much use to his hens). What is important though, is that he can hold his own with his wives, many of them generations his senior, otherwise he'll be henpecked. And spending time hiding in the house under the kitchen table, won't cut any ice with them.

Allow me to introduce the rest of the hens. Our *dramatis personae:* in charge of the flock is the Nasty Hen, a small elderly black bantam crossbred from farmyard stock, still laying despite her venerable 8 years of age; next, her deputy – *grande dame* of the Orpingtons, the Very Old Hen, who bears a marked resemblance to the breed's late patron, the Queen Mother; followed by the Old Hen and her Daughter, inseparable and like two peas in a pod. Next in line comes

4

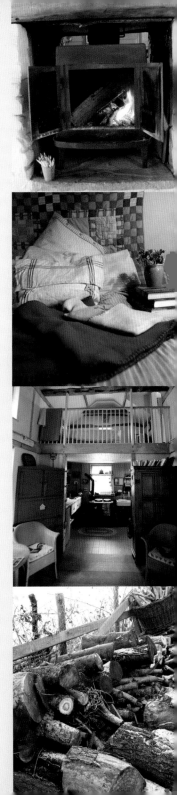

the V.O Hen's offspring, born last year and my Best Layer, rather overshadowed by the Beauty, whose name says it all. At the bottom of the pecking order and subsequently always hanging about the peripheries of the gang is last year's Pullet, a dear little girlie, who is sure to move up the ranks as she starts to lay.

With howling gales and low light levels, these ladies and their new consorts are lounging about out of the wind, preening – but they're not laying. They're missing that wondrous beam from the sun, to come and reach that particular part of their brain, activating the hormones to trigger their production of eggs. That same beam we all need to ward off the winter blues. No wonder bed is the most tempting place to be at this time of the year.

Our marriage bed, bought in monthly instalments from Heal's in 1976, boasts an orthopaedic mattress (the puritan in me can't cope with soft bedding) and is home to cotton-filled duvets, pillows and bolsters, special friends developed over years of trial and error. All are housed on a platform over the Rayburn, warm and toasty, with telly and radio, reading light and piles of books. The cat and I have to make a supreme effort not to go to bed before supper.

2th

Tomorrow, my elder son, gorgeous Jacques and his girlfriend Saskia, go travelling – again. An essential rite of passage nowadays, and I don't begrudge them for an instant, but this is the *second* time, and like most parents, I'm pleased they're going, but much happier when they get back. This time it's for work and they're heading to New Zealand to work as a model-maker and stylist respectively, visiting the rest of the Far East on their way there and back.

6th

I can't bear to see them off, and am left, staring morosely at all their belongings, wondering where on earth to store all this stuff. In an effort to raise my spirits, I brave the elements and grab the lawn rake. Brisk sweeping – that good old stoic recipe for all ills. The least movement in the garden attracts the hens. Soon, I'm surrounded by great blobs of damp – but bright feathers – the colour of sunshine. And their eternal optimism that my travails will turn up something for them to eat, helps my big brassy ladies and I work ourselves into a chirpier mood.

So, it's my younger son Max and me, together again. He's back from college in London and looking for work-experience locally as a sound engineer. It's been a while since I've shared the house, but I'm looking forward to having my lovely Max – and his music – back again.

7th

The Christmas decorations always get put away long before Twelfth Night, and the house looks bare. I love its tidy minimalism, but miss the natural charm of living greenery. I killed off all the house plants long ago, and even the conservatory can't sustain any higher form of plant life than the house leek, but indoor winter bulbs are easy. The paper white narcissi planted in glass containers are fresh and elegant, even though their perfume in excess reminds me slightly of rotting meat, followed by white hyacinths, sometimes twenty to a dozen in a huge pot, and then amaryllis (now known as hippeastrum). I have three greenish 'Lemon Lime' and their fat buds are snaking their way up lustily, like speeded-up time-lapse photography. They spend their dormant summer holidays in the shady part of the conservatory, kept meanly watered and fed, in the hope they may repeat their fakir-like performance next year.

Next on stage is a big yellow enamel bucket, chock-full of exotic cymbidium orchids. Green budded and pot-bound, they live half the year in a shady part of the garden, four months in the conservatory out of the frost and two, flowering their socks off exotically in the coolest part of the dining room. Apart from a little seaweed feed in the summer, they seem rewardingly independent and indestructible.

8th

Time to put a few New Year's resolutions into practice.
Resolution 1.
A recent article about my fat blonde hens showed a photo of their fat blonde owner that sent me scurrying to the scales. I weigh myself occasionally, and hadn't noticed much change. So I put on my specs (they shouldn't weigh much) and the needle's halfway position between the stones hadn't changed, but to my horror, the amount of stones had.

So this morning, after a frugal breakfast of a few porridge oats, a sprinkle of ground flax seeds, a walnut, some grated pear with a dusting of cinnamon, soaked in a drop of water, I'm off pounding the lane, joining the rest of the nation in an effort to lose weight. At mid-morning I'm allowed some pumpkin seeds, at lunchtime a mixed salad with soaked black-eyed beans and a boiled egg – or a tin of sardines or mackerel, for tea a piece of fruit and for supper a bowl of broth or miso (the most palatable is by Clearspring). And pints of water, with perhaps the odd cup of tea (Dragonfly Rooibos Earl Grey).The quantities may in fact be a little more generous – but that in essence is my regime for the next few months.

Resolution 2.
Personally, the most important, is regular exercise. All my family: maternal grandmother, father and elder son suffer from excess adrenalin. Although outwardly we may seem a pudding-like lot, underneath really does beat a racing heart. We suffer shaky hands and sleepless nights unless we desist from caffeine, sugar and sloth. All my favourites. My natural routine peaks from running or swimming 5 times a week to trough-like days wasted playing spider solitaire ('difficult' level, admittedly) on the computer.

Resolution 3.
To spend a little time every day gardening and not let the months slip through my fingers, with the result that I'm always working in a hurry to prepare for a photo shoot, or a course, or an open day. To make work outside an enjoyable recreation, not a panic inducing chore.

Resolution 4.
To try to eat seasonally, locally and consume less animal protein. According to the Food Standards Agency, women need 40 grams of protein a day and men, 50. We can hardly complain about exploitative animal farming methods if we

encourage over-production by endlessly buying the end products. Incidentally, an egg supplies us with 6 grams of protein. By eating more fruit and veg, we combat the consequences of age-induced diseases by bolstering our natural defences. I'm going to make home-grown produce, which is full of therapeutic properties, a major part of my diet, backed up by farmers' market and farm-gate suppliers and locally sourced food from the better supermarkets.

So: eat less and local, and exercise more and relax. A pretty predictable wish list.

10th

A call from the producer of Radio 4's Food Programme, asking me to come up to town and comment on air about backyard hen keepers' fears concerning the growing bird flu crisis, puts things back into perspective and galvanizes me to action. I have been planning some sort of on-line information network to keep hen keepers up-to-date with news specific to them. And above all, to lobby the government to allow us to vaccinate our small backyard flocks against this worrying disease.

The press and authorities thunder on, God knows, we all hope nothing will come of it, and I realize, globally, this is a much larger problem than saving a few pet hens, but I'm worried our birds may fall victim to well intentioned bureaucracy, rather than the disease itself, and be sacrificed in some fevered cleansing exercise by the men in white (as were many perfectly healthy animals during the foot-and-mouth epidemic).

Practically, what can we do to protect our hens? According to Defra, the threat will come from wild birds, via their faeces, so we should keep feed and water containers away from this source and, in the event of an outbreak, make contingency plans to keep our birds undercover. As a short-term measure this should not be a problem. Long-term it would affect the health and wellbeing of our flocks and make them even more susceptible to disease.

So, appointments are made with website designers and all the professionals involved, to set up the Henkeepers' Association.

12th

Setting up an association is much more complicated than I'd assumed. The website design is straightforward enough, though expensive, because we want to be able to update it ourselves. I say, we. Allow me to introduce my techie - Max. Thank heavens he's here. I am totally the wrong generation to understand all this technospeak. But have made myself useful designing a logo, preparing the text for the home page, and working on content for the other sections. Should we have a page listing recommended products, a monthly diary, a list of useful poultry books and magazines, a section on feeding? Obviously there should be a large news section. Turn down the idea of a forum. Too complicated to monitor.

I've been advised to set up a limited company, so legal advice is imperative apparently. I don't understand why we need to protect ourselves in this way. I'd have thought with a disclaimer that none of our advice is case specific, but professionals are so careful, and I don't have the confidence to disagree.

Discover the complications involved in setting up a company are overwhelming. We have to nominate company officials, I will have to pay PAYE, and since the association is not a real association but an information network.........

15th

Spend a day winding down and cooling my temper in the garden, sweeping leaves, and cutting back plants that are overhanging the edges of the beds to protect the lawn, taking care not to disturb habitats or remove any seedheads that the varied inhabitants of the garden might enjoy. In a short, relaxing walk round the plot, I marvel at the cascades of catkins, the bulbs up already and the viburnums, flowering their socks off. Who for, I wonder? Well advanced, a couple of hellebores are already in flower, while others barely pierce the soil. Pick a few to float on a plate, so we can see their hidden faces, prettier than pansies and more than welcome.

As I go to feed them, the ducks don't recognize me in my new orange beret, and rush back across the road hungry, to their winter quarters.

Dusk falls, and I pull a few leeks from the spectral vegetable garden. I love my blue green 'Natan' or 'Blue Willa' leeks or the almost purple 'St Victor'. Grown from pencil thick seedlings, that start life on a window sill in February, then graduate into the conservatory to be planted out in April. Later successional plantings take me almost through the year. I cut their roots and tops off straight on to the compost heap, to avoid bringing the garden, literally, into the house.

Placed in the low, shallow sink, they are cleaned by slicing half way through the leaves lengthways and splayed under running water to dislodge any grit. Then sliced with a handful of dried, soaked Borlotti beans* to make this warming Leek and Dried Bean Minestrone.

First, fry the leeks in a little goosefat, then add a pint/600ml of stock and simmer the beans with a bayleaf till soft (about 45 minutes). Serve with a drizzle of fruity olive oil, some chopped parsley or chervil, and a grating of cheese.

I eat leeks steamed with red peppers with a dressing of sesame oil, a dash of soy sauce, chopped ginger and pared lemon zest, or blanched when young in place of salad onions. Leeks tick all the boxes: tasty, easy to grow and they look stunning in the plot.

*If you grow your own Borlotti beans (I love 'Lingua di Fuoco' – Tongues of Fire) in much the same way as runner beans, they can be frozen immediately after harvesting: this obviates the need for overnight soaking.

19th

Wake to a landscape hidden by a blanket of snow and an email with attachment from the happy couple, holidaying in Sri Lanka. First egg from my youngest pullet. The turn in the weather doesn't cool the drakes' ardour. Out in the village, the ducks are already pairing up. Troston is home to a huge surplus of drakes. Would anyone like a few? Each female has attracted at least three *beaux*, not counting the

cabal of disreputable louts who hang around the feeding station, on the off-chance of a gang-bang with any poor hungry female as she lands.

20th

Sit reading with my feet up on the stove. My Rayburn is an old friend. Bought way back in the late seventies to celebrate the birth of our firstborn and accentuate hearth and home, it snuggled just a little too cosily in our small London kitchen. So, transported here with great muscle and expense, and fed extravagantly on oil, it now gives heart to the house, heats the bathwater, dries, airs and sort-of-irons the clothes, and cooks the food.

Less glamorous than its iconic Scandinavian sister the Aga, the British designed Rayburn was launched in 1946 (the year of my birth). Initially over 1500 a week were produced, many of which are probably still to be found in kitchens today. Ours has a smart, matt black cast iron finish, and looks its best wiped clean with an olive oily rag. It chugs away throughout the winter months, warming the open plan kitchen and living area, and the platform bedroom above it, like the plate warmer on an old fashioned cooker.

Rayburn cookery takes some getting used to. The hottest part of the top oven is on the right side, so dishes need to be turned at half time; the temperature drops fairly dramatically every time you open the door; and though there is a thermostat that can be adjusted, the effect is far from instantaneous. You have to learn to plan ahead. Memories of my early sweaty failures still make me smart.

Soups are foolproof though, whatever you cook on. Simply, the basic recipe involves lightly frying a selection of veg and herbs of your choice in a little oil, butter or goosefat till coated and then diluting with stock. For speed, I suggest Marigold powdered granules or soaked dried mushroom liquor (but you can of course, make your own base from onions, carrots, celery, and a bouquet garni with leftover vegetable trimmings). When the vegetables have softened, season and then liquidize. I recommend my little Bamix hand-held mixer, it's so quick to use and easy to clean.

This hearty Winter Soup will warm and cheer the blues away, and uses garden veg, such as celeriac that over-winters underground, and squashes that will store if kept in a cool place.

Lightly fry a sliced onion or leek and a large clove of garlic in a little butter and olive oil in a large soup pan. Peel and roughly chop ½ a butternut squash and half a celeriac root. Put in the pan with 2 chopped pears (they don't have to be your best). Stir till lightly browned, adding 2 pints/1.2 litres of stock and a glass of white wine. Spice it up with a cinnamon stick, a few cloves and a bayleaf. Simmer till soft.

Pick out the floating spices before liquidizing, adding a little more stock if too thick. Serve with a whirl of cream (not for me, I'm on a diet) a squeeze of lemon juice and this delicious topping.

Fry a few chopped sage leaves in butter, till brown and crispy (take care, they soon turn black and burnt). Add to soups, or to a plate of plain boiled pasta with a grating of parmesan and a little black pepper.

Butternut squash benefits from a long sunny growing season. The variety 'Butternut Sprinter' is an early cropper. Try these pretty Timbales with a Red Pepper Sauce for a starter or light lunch.

Bake a squash in the oven till tender with three red peppers for the sauce. Remove the seeds from the squash, scoop out the flesh and process till smooth. Place in a pan with ¼ pt/450ml crème fraîche until the mixture thickens. Leave to cool. Whisk in three eggs gradually. Season with salt, pepper and a little nutmeg. Spoon the mixture into 4 well buttered timbales or moulds, and place in a roasting pan full of boiling water in the oven for about 45 minutes till firm.

De-seed and peel the roasted peppers and blend with a clove of garlic, a tablespoon of balsamic vinegar and 3 tablespoons each of tomato puree and olive oil. Warm before spooning round the timbales and garnish with chervil or parsley.

I grow celeriac (variety 'Monarch') from seed in pots undercover to plant outside in May. It appreciates a damp spot and a warm blanket of mulch in autumn.

To make a sprightly salad, boil the peeled, chopped celeriac in salty water with two tablespoons of white wine vinegar to stop discoloration. When soft, strain and slice finely, using the reduced liquor to make a dressing with oil, chopped shallots, or young leeks and a few celeriac leaves. Season well. This vinaigrette will go deliciously gelatinous and keeps for a week in the fridge.

I'm allowed an extra portion, because I've lost 6 lbs. Even for those who can eat puddings, there's little joy to be found in the garden yet. We have to rely on those stalwarts of the fruit bowl, the apples, pears and bananas. Looking forward to harvesting the rhubarb, snug under its cloche. Until then, I make do with a delicious Christmas present, lucky me - a jar of prunes steeped in brandy with a twist of lemon peel.

Delicious drained with a little Greek yoghurt or mascarpone cheese. Or dried apricots, soaked overnight in some weak Earl Grey tea, and then fooled with cream and a stripped vanilla pod. But this was only for guests of course. I just had stewed fruit.

My American friend Carol has offered me her recipe for Caramel Apple Charlotte:

First cook the caramel by melting 6oz/175g sugar in a pan with 2 tablespoons of lemon juice and 2 teaspoons of water, taking care not to let it overcook and go dark. Make an apple purée with 1½ lb/700g apples, and 6oz/175g muscovado sugar, a knob of butter, the grated rind of a lemon or orange, spiced with cinnamon and a few cloves.

Cut some good bread, or better still some brioche, into small slices and dip them in the caramel and line a well-buttered ovenproof mould or dish. Spoon in the fruit, top with a layer of bread, and pour over the rest of the caramel. Cook in a medium oven till hot – about 15 minutes,

depending on the size of the dish. Allow to stand before turning out and sprinkle with icing sugar. Or just serve, straight from the dish if too sticky. I ate this fruity caramel delight chez Carol, before Christmas, made with pears. No wonder I've put on weight.

29th

Website progressing slowly. Bureaucracy driving me berserk. With more outbreaks of bird flu in Turkey, and hundreds of phone calls and emails asking for advice, I'm keen to get on-line, but we are waiting for articles of association or something and costs are mounting. The leader of the Parish Council has accused me of putting the health of the community at risk, by occasionally letting my hens into the house.

I'm walking on eggshells and realizing how fragile my livelihood is. Unable to control anything, it's like living in a house of cards. One little puff of trouble and it will all come tumbling down.

31st

A brisk walk up the lane to clear my head. The ditches are blocked again. Disowned by local authority and farmers alike, who is supposed to keep the lane from flooding, as the water cascades along the roads into the village? Pick up a bough or two from a fallen ash tree along the verge. We'll have plenty of kindling now. The word goes out; like Cornish wreckers, within a week there'll be no sign of this giant that's been rotting vertically for decades.

Trudging through a sea of mud, I can pick out ponies' hoof marks – probably made by my god daughter who often trots over to see me, mixed with the boot tracks of hundreds of squaddies from the local military camp, who pummel this circuit for exercise, sometimes in full kit. My heart breaks for them. They're just boys, much younger than my sons. I wonder if they understand what they have let themselves into.

To bed early, feeling unwell. Too much dieting and inner turmoil. Our immune systems eavesdrop on our internal dialogues and react to all our problems. I need time to remind myself of the good things in life.

FEB*ruary*

Cockcrow

Brassicas

Hellebores

Frosty Mornings

Pancake Day

Seville Marmalade

St. Valentine's Day

1st

Church Cottage was built on the verge, by the side of the lane on land traditionally available free of charge to those who settled there. Evident on parish maps as an unnamed building of some sort in the mid 18th century, there was probably always something here, given its position opposite the huge wool church. The house is built of local brick – from the clay pit up the lane, and flint from the fields – to just hip height, like all agricultural buildings around here. The rest of the original walls are a fragile carapace – a few hazel twigs covered with daubed clay and horsehair. No wonder the biting winds whistle through. I'm saving up to clapboard the north face, with modern insulating fabric sandwiched in between.

Inside, half the cottage goes up to rafter height, while the other side has two low ceilinged stories with windows at ankle level on the upper floors, and two flights of stairs. Unconventionally designed, with much of the space open-plan, we built on east and west wings with a long conservatory in between. This house has magically suited us, first as a weekend cottage, and thereafter as a family home with growing offspring. Nowadays it divides pretty neatly in two, offering Max a flat with studio space and bathroom (share kitchen) and most miraculous of all, the sound of his music system – originally decks of equipment with terrifying electrical output, now just a neat computer/keyboard combo – is muffled by efficient soundproofing. So we'll rub along till he finds a full-time job and flies the coop.

2nd

A few snowdrops are flowering. Their meek demeanour reminds me of the first time I crossed the threshold of this cottage in February 25 years ago. The sale was completed the day before Max was born, so I had been otherwise engaged, and made my first visit with a tiny baby in a carrier worn inside my jumper to keep him warm and protect him from the freezing northerly winds. Our Norfolk builders were retiling the roof, and my husband, a French Canadian couldn't understand a word they said. So I had come down as interpreter.

Fighting my way briskly up the lane to restart my circulation, I met an old lady, who told me quite definitely that we would not like this spot. To this day, I have no idea who she was. I'd have liked to meet her again to tell her how wrong she proved to be.

4th

Max has been invaluable helping launch the Henkeepers' Association website, most of which is incomprehensible to me. It's all done by email, nothing face-to-face. A phone call from my bank who are wondering why I'm bothering to set up a company at all, so now I'm getting conflicting advice left, right and centre. I try to concentrate on my contribution to the site, and will sort the rest out later.

Email from my friend Alma in Holland. The Dutch poultry organizations and press have been pressurizing their government for preventative vaccination since 40 million birds were slaughtered in an outbreak of avian flu three years ago. Write to Bill Wiggins, shadow Minister for Agriculture, who keeps hens and has promised to table a

series of parliamentary questions from us to Margaret Beckett. Hen keepers are worried, lots of calls.

Try to distract myself with an afternoon's toil among the vegetables. Given the paucity of pleasures to be found there, it's not surprising that February was chosen to host the start of Lent and all its wintry sacrifices. But, unvisited in their frosty quarantine, the crinkly blue-green Savoy cabbages, elegantly ribbed purple 'January Kings' and multicoloured kales, started in pots last summer, are now a luscious tapestry, especially when frosted with their outer leaves nibbled to lace by the hens.

Forget those memories of school dinner cabbage, the brassica family provides lots of vitamin-rich, low calorie restoratives that we all crave and need at this time of the year, after the largesse of Christmas. Kale and cabbage needs either speedy Oriental steaming and stir frying, or slow simmering in soups and minestrones. Leaves can be eaten raw if you wash them thoroughly, checking for grit and pests, and then pat dry with a tea towel. Here are a few of my hand picked suggestions:

Cavolo Nero is a navy blue palm tree of kale, which looks especially stunning if underplanted with pot marigolds.

Its top leaves can be harvested now, cut into ribbons and stir fried with pancetta, sundried tomatoes and pine nuts, then dressed with a few drops of soy sauce and sesame oil.

33

Equally exotic are the crinkled burgundy curly kales ('Redbor' is a favourite of mine).

Their tiny top leaves will liven up any winter salad, especially if partnered with chopped olives and feta cheese, and dressed with a warming blend of fresh ginger, two tablespoons each of lemon juice and sesame oil, and one of soy sauce and rice vinegar. Sprinkle with sesame seeds and chopped spring onions.

Have you ever tried red cabbage raw in a pretty pink coleslaw?

Finely shred quarter of a cabbage with a bread knife, and chop an apple. Dress with a mixture of one part yoghurt to one part sour cream, with crushed juniper berries and pink peppercorns, seasoned and sprinkled with chopped parsley.

And for those of us trying to lose weight, cabbage makes a diet-conscious alternative to pasta.

Sliced thinly and steamed like tagliatelli, serve with a tomato sauce, topped with parmesan cheese, or use whole leaves like sheets of lasagna or cannelloni. First steam a few large leaves, fill with a mixture of cooked rice, pine nuts, chopped leeks and soaked dried mushrooms, and bind with beaten egg. Then roll up the leaf, secure with a cocktail stick and steam for 10 minutes, seasoned with salt, pepper and grated nutmeg.

10th

A burst of unseasonal warmth encourages me to leave the computer for the day to blitz the garden. I realize my instincts to tidy should be curbed. Old stems and foliage are essential, not just as frost protection for young growth, but to protect habitat and food sources for birds and insects. But surely the buddleias could be cut down, as well as the late fruiting raspberries and the gooseberries could be pruned? I know it's a little premature to be cutting back the climbing roses that grow against the house, but today coincides with the monthly visit from Keith, who helps with garden jobs I can't manage alone. The offer of his extendable ladder just can't be refused. So I hold the ladder steady, and point out the branches to be pruned while he cuts, swaying above me precariously as I dodge the falling prickly offcuts.

11th

Keith has returned with his son to cut down the chestnut tree I foolishly planted from a sprouted conker in the meadow. Now a substantial tree, and a potential source of deathly shade for the entire garden, we have made the sad decision it will have to go. The awful sound of the chain saw cuts right through me as I sweep up the debris, and Keith chops up the major boughs for the woodpile, stacking them to dry till next year and filling the huge basket with logs for the house.

Later, a small bonfire in the veg garden augurs the end of the conker tree. Moodily, watching the ashes in the gloaming, I finish off the brandy leftover from the jar of prunes, and listen to the little owls in the woods across the field.

14th

St Valentine's is the day hens traditionally start to lay after their winter break. The weather is mild, daylight hours are lengthening, and there's plenty to eat. The Pullet, hatched late last summer laid her first egg three weeks ago and the others have produced sporadically. Reward your ladies with mixed grains and seeds, especially flax, pumpkins and sunflower seeds, available from your feed merchant. Seeds are rich in omega 3 oils, making them good for your birds and through their eggs, good for you too. A little cod liver oil in their breakfast of moistened wholemeal bread will add the vitamin D that's missing through lack of sunshine.

Open the post late to find a letter bearing the House of Commons' familiar crest. Inside are our written Parliamentary replies. No, the government will not use vaccination as a weapon against H5N1. The rest is just a repetition of Defra's advice on bio-security techniques, which have been designed for hens kept in batteries.

It's pointless to keep food and water undercover, away from wild birds if your flock then promptly go out into the garden and drink from the first puddle or upturned leaf they find, and peck at plants, insects and soil that may have been infected by wild bird droppings anyway. It would be sad to stop encouraging songbirds into the garden, by withdrawing bird food, and probably make them all the more likely to pinch the hens' feed. Fairly intractable problems, and none of us wants the only solution to be penning our hens undercover.

Have contacted fruitcage manufacturers to see if there might be a dual purpose solution to keeping my flock safe, maybe adding a solid plastic roof. Find a home golf range that would certainly offer plenty of space, but at £700 is quite an investment and would probably blow away in the slightest breeze. Some of the henhouse builders are

advertising covered runs, offering very restricted space, I'm sure my flock would get very argumentative in such cramped conditions. And the Cockerel would definitely need some kind of batchelor pad annexed onto the main run.

The problem is solved for those with barns, spare garages or stables. They could replace doors and windows with netting, but am sceptical that a polytunnel, even with huge ventilation panels, will be the answer to any poultry maiden's prayer.

New stationery is delivered. It is incorrect, so returned. Can't wait. Work late, sending out our first press releases on hand headed writing paper. Wonder if all my contacts in the press who've written pretty pieces about us in magazines over the years will take up this story? Not a very sexy subject.

17th

Up listening to the news at the crack of dawn. The H5N1 virus has been found in mute swans in Baltic Germany, rather close to home. German poultry keepers are ordered to keep all birds under cover. A message from Alma: she has started to round up her beloved flock of bantam Wyandottes, and kindly wishes this awful business doesn't reach us.

Three French *départements* are vaccinating without permission from Brussels. Good for them. Write again to all the Defra ministers: Beckett, Bradshaw and Bach, but they are on half term till the 27th. Feel very frustrated.

A welcome distraction, a visit from my friend Barbara, bearing gifts – a jar from her new batch of Seville marmalade. And a copy of her acclaimed recipe which I pass on to you.

To make 5lbs/2.25kg of the best marmalade I've ever tasted: Scrub 1½lb/700g of Seville oranges and one unwaxed lemon. Place in a pan with 2pts/1.2litres of water, cover and simmer for two hours.

Remove the fruit from the pan with a slotted spoon, and halve. Scoop out the pips, flesh (and some of the pith from the lemon, if thick). Return all this to the pan.

Boil the pips for 5 minutes to extract the pectin, and then fish them out. Using a sharp knife and fork, slice the peel into thin or chunky strips. Combine juice, fruit, peel and 3lb/1.35kg of granulated sugar in the pan. Stir till sugar has dissolved. Bring to the boil and boil rapidly for 30-35 minutes until it reaches setting point.

Remove from the heat, stir gently to disperse the froth.
Leave to stand for 5 minutes to prevent the fruit rising.
Transfer to warmed sterilised jars and seal.

Try using Seville oranges in place of lemons for a welcome change in these dishes: combine their juice with walnut oil and honey to dress an uplifting winter salad of oranges, watercress and chicory; and try our recipe for lemon curd in April's chapter substituting lemons with Seville oranges.

19th

The Henkeepers' Association goes online. Membership £25.00 for five years.

20th

Appear on BBC News Look East at 6 and 10pm. Long piece on launch of association. The Buff Orps look magnificent in their new plumage. I look dreadful - cold and worried. Pretty much sums me up.

21st

First members enrol. Loads of interest. Spending too much time on the computer. As I walk the length of the house from office to kitchen, to stretch my legs and make a large cup of tea to warm my fingers, I pass two large windows that look out on to the lane. I'm not a fan of net curtains and blinds would hide an old familiar friend – the view of the church wall, so the desultory few passers by, the dog walkers and ramblers have an uninterrupted view of us. (Not the joggers, they'll be moving too fast).

In an effort to preserve a little privacy, we've put up three or four narrow shelves, in line with the main glazing bars and they house collections of odds and ends to distract the eye: a set of painted Peruvian tin chickens, groupings of little lead animals from old toy farmyards, photographs, postcards and family memorabilia. Most villagers have the decency to avert their eyes, and the fact that I rarely clean the windows must be a slight deterrent, but occasionally you catch inquisitive stares and peering faces.

22nd

Letter is published in The Daily Telegraph:

Dear Sir,

In the light of recent developments in Holland and the comments of Sir David King, The Henkeepers' Association would encourage Defra to allow preventative vaccination as part of the fight against avian flu.

The Dutch multi-pronged attack including vaccination of free range and 'poultry held in private hands' is based on valuable experience of widespread bird flu during 2003. Surely we can learn from their experiences?

David King's prediction that we are likely to be prone to this disease for five years plus, begs the question; does Defra intend to eradicate all poultry over that period?

Up to 250,000 private hen keepers keep birds in their gardens. They are not transported around the country, seldom sold or exhibited, and cannot fly. They are rarely killed for food and cannot practicably be kept under cover in humane conditions.

We urge Defra to take our views into account when formulating future policy.

Yours faithfully
Francine Raymond
The Henkeepers' Association.

We are asked to join Elm Farm Organic Research Centre as joint signatories to a letter to Margaret Beckett. Martin

Gurdon, a motoring journalist/hen keeper who has written books on his experiences with poultry, gets me in the BBC loop. Start to network with all the other poultry groups and breed clubs. Good response from the press, with a column in Country Life and small pieces printed or promised in the rest.

24th

High winds have blown open the doors to the summer house, and the hens have forsaken the verandah and moved inside to sit on the stored deckchairs and garden furniture. Perched precariously on a metal table, lord of all he surveys, stands the new Cockerel, now in sole charge of his harem.

It isn't essential to keep a cock with your hens, in fact it's not even advisable if you are a beginner; have small children; or neighbours who don't appreciate the early morning alarm calls. Hens will lay without the assistance or otherwise of a mate, he's only needed if you want the eggs to be fertile.

Cockcrow (currently 5.45am) is a magical time in the morning and a special part of country life. If it's too early, one just makes a mental note, turns over and goes back to sleep. I suppose though, if you have other worries, or unresolved problems with your neighbours, it could become a bone of contention. In fact, in response to increasing numbers of disputes about crowing reported to District Councils throughout the countryside and suburbia, the Poultry Club has issued a series of guidelines:

Think carefully, do you need a cock with your hens?

You certainly don't need more than one.

Make sure your poultry house is as far away from neighbours and as lightproof as possible. Your birds still need adequate ventilation though.

Shut your birds in at night and keep them in till 7am.

Explain your hobby to your neighbours, invite them to see your birds.

A present of a dozen eggs always goes down well.

Co-operate with the Environmental Health Officer and explain the efforts you're making to deal with the noise.

Invite your District Councillor round and show him your set up. And keep your cool.

Fortunately, during the last 15 years my neighbours have been models of patience, or else very heavy sleepers, and this cockerel emits a strange, quiet three note crow. Checking him over, I notice he needs a little assistance with his *toilette*. Whoever designed the Orpington (I know it was William Cook, in Kent in 1860) got it fundamentally wrong. They are nowadays bred so big, they can't reach their *derrières* to preen.

Usually a little delicate intervention with a pair of blunt-ended scissors will remove any soiled feathers, but for this and many pure breeds, a life unchecked on the open range is not entirely appropriate. Those breeds with exaggerated muffling, beards, crests and pom-poms, may need a little hairdressing to view life unhindered. Cocks with massive wattles could get frostbite – a problem cured by judicious applications of petroleum jelly, and any breed with excessive footings or very long tails will need attention when their surroundings are muddy.

Of course, it is important to keep the weird and wonderful characteristics of the pure breeds, not just for aesthetic and historical reasons, but also so commercial breeders can dip into their gene pools for Frankenstein hybridising. But I do wish breeders wouldn't exaggerate – this is not Crufts. Orpingtons are now bred too big for their own good, it makes them susceptible to heart disease – not to mention the other problem.

Move a few straw bales to offer more shelter in the run, and nail a small piece of carpet over their pophole for extra protection against draughts. Hens are well-insulated against the cold with their fine duvet jackets, but hate the wind ruffling their feathers. Max and I turn the henhouse round so the entrance faces away from the prevailing wind. Hope they manage to find their front door as light fades and they go to roost in their newspaper insulated *palais des poulets*, and sleep soundly through the night on the antics of celebrities and politicians.

26th

A visit from Health and Safety. Fortunately, an appointment was made, and the house has been blitzed. I'm afraid this kitchen will never be up to their standards, with its ancient wooden surfaces, old ceramic sink and open shelves. Though small, the area is quite functional with all the major working zones - fridge, cooker and sink within arm's length of one another. I've never lusted after an all singing all dancing fitted kitchen, with banks of cupboards housing rarely used equipment you can't find. The larder and a few shelves are all I need. Luckily our café menu is very basic, so our opportunity to poison is limited. We serve tea and cakes, with my cake baker, Rena baking from home, and no meat or fish – red rags to hygiene officers. But you can never take anything for granted, so the eating area has been scrubbed almost bare.

I have bought spanking new plastic cake boxes, a range of cleaning materials the ecologist in me frowns on, and a fridge thermometer. Pieces of furniture I never thought of as free-standing were moved, windows cleaned and I look pretty spic and span myself. The jolly official is slightly bemused by the whole set up, writes Very Low Risk on her forms and leaves immediately, saying someone will be back in five years. And she never even opened the fridge to see my lovely thermometer.

Five years ago the previous officer took one look at the catering facilities, said, 'yes well that's health, let's go and look at safety' and we went off together into the garden to discuss the dangers of small children falling into the pond. So I've been very lucky.

28th

Shrove Tuesday – Pancake Day. Make a special meal to cheer us with a naughty treat to celebrate the enrolment of our 33rd member. Thin pancakes wrapped around delicious Halva ice cream and drizzled with honey. As sweetmeats go, halva has at least the saving grace to be made of health-giving ground sesame seeds and nuts.

Beat 3 egg yolks until pale and creamy. Take a large pot of single cream and heat in a saucepan to just below boiling point. Pour the cream carefully into the egg yolks, whisking as you go. Return to the heat, stir until custardy, then crumble in 8oz/250g of best halva. Allow to cool, then freeze, removing from the freezer to the fridge half an hour before needed.

Meanwhile prepare your pancake batter. Beat an egg, adding 3fl oz/75ml single cream and the same of water.

When blended, add 2oz /55g of plain flour and whisk until perfectly smooth, adding a tablespoonful of sugar. Leave to rest.

Heat a knob of butter in medium sized pan. When foaming hot, pour on a small ladleful of batter, tilting the pan to spread the mixture evenly. Flip the pancake as it cooks. Stack, covered with foil to keep warm, then roll your crêpes with a filling of ice cream and drizzle with warmed honey.

Sweet crêpes can be filled with apple purée and cinnamon, or marmalade and marzipan, or any good jam or jelly with whipped cream. Savoury pancakes can be made with chickpea or buckwheat flour and filled with ricotta and greens, with mushrooms and gruyère or goat's cheese and pesto.

To decorate the table, I pick a few hellebore flowers from each hybrid variety and float them on a large plate. The range of colours and markings are stunning. What a pity they usually hide their pretty faces so modestly.

51

MARCH

Sorrel

Rhubarb

Henhouses

Garden Birds

March Winds

Seed Catalogues

Hen Keeping Courses

1st

Our plot is quite small – in all about $^2/_3$ of an acre. We bought the cottage with a narrow strip of garden raised two foot higher than the house, backing on to open fields, and two other small gardens surrounded by low curved patchwork brick and flint walls at either end. All we found were a fine apple tree, an overgrown perimeter hedge, boasting a truncated lime, (probably a seedling from the churchyard opposite), an ash, and a couple of Dutch Elm diseased saplings. An inner hedge of pink roses flowered their socks off in summer and a carpet of snowdrops paved the areas close to house in the springtime. The soil is mostly clay with a sandy seam on the western edge.

A pretty blank canvas. I spent the first few years, frustrated with tiny children and a year in plaster after a bad car accident, endlessly drawing plans on paper, visiting local nurseries and fantasizing my way through plant lists. I managed a few beds, a square of yews, a walnut tree and swathes of 'Albertine' roses. Four seemingly endless years later we moved here permanently and extended the house. We were exceptionally lucky to able to buy more garden land, admittedly at an exorbitant price, from the farmer.

So then we were proud possessors of a venerable oak on the eastern perimeter, enough space for a drive and garage/workshop, room for a much longed-for pond, an extension to the yew hedge from a square to an avenue, and of my neighbour's abandoned vegetable garden, more than doubling our original acreage.

To cut down the effect of the biting winds and to preserve a little privacy we kept all the old boundaries and that's why the garden is still divided into 10 small sections: to the east; a yard, the drive, the cut flower garden, the 'badminton court', the meadow and pond, in the centre; the perennial garden and the avenue, and on the west hand side sits the vegetable plot, chicken run and the tiny secret garden.

2nd

An untidy pile of seed catalogues has been gathering dust on my bedside table since the beginning of the year. Dog-eared, they've been pored over, shuffled and scribbled on, as I've visualised and planned my vegetable plot and rotation of crops, over and over again. It takes the first portents of spring to galvanize me into action and order my seeds.

I escape among the pictures, the packets and the sound they make when you shake them, and especially inside the pages of this year's favourite catalogue from Seeds of Italy. Hidden away among a treasure trove of luscious tomatoes, Venetian asparagus, and red garlic 'Rosso di Sulmona' are mouth watering gems: purple artichokes, waiting to be marinaded; cream aubergines or egg plants, some smooth and cream like the eggs they're named after; and erba stella, agretti and small leaved mustard to enhance summer salads. I spot a black fig 'Borgiotto', suited to our cooler climes, that I could eat sandwiched between crumbled goat's cheese and rashers of bacon, and a range of truffle bearing hazel bushes. Sweet dreams of harvests with fantasy meals to follow.

Greedily, I tick order forms for generous packets of 'Borrettana' onion seeds, so I can pickle the little flat onions in rich balsamic vinegar, like they do in expensive delicatessens. I add a selection of multi-coloured Borlotti and Cannellini beans with romantic names, like old fashioned roses, to dry off for winter soups, and then plump for courgette 'Zucchini da Fiore' that produces only flowers that never fruit, so I can fry them in olive oil dipped in a little light batter. As an afterthought I include a packet of pumpkin 'Zucca da Marmellata' to make jam just like the owner's Aunt Angelina.

Other technicolour catalogues tempt me with broad bean 'Violetta', whose purply hue will keep if lightly steamed; Swiss chard 'Bright Lights' to add colour to the beds and to our salads, and a range of Tuscan and Provencal saladini. Suffolk Herbs offer a wide range of Oriental vegetables and I'm tempted by 'Tatsoi', a strange rosette of tiny tender leaves and an optimistic range of healthy sprouting seeds, complete with sprouters and visions of continuing weight loss.

I would also like another quince tree, but in the end I settle for Damson 'Merryweather' which will crop young, with blue/black fruit and dusky bloom for pies, jams and future vintages of damson gin.

4th

All those familiar migrating birds, much loved portents of the seasons; the first swallow skimming the pond, and sipping the greenish water or picking beakfuls of mud to build her nest, the heartstopping V's of geese on our vast skies, even the cuckoo now herald anxieties and can't be sure of a warm welcome, especially if they've spent their winter holidays in Africa. Am feeding the wild birds at the far end of the garden away from my flock. I have always loved birds. Their perpetual optimism is astounding. Despite the vagaries of the weather, depredations by predators and loss of habitat, how often must they wonder, is it worth it? I admire their built-in determination to just start again and keep going. From my desk I can see a tree creeper, like a little mouse, working the apple tree bark through the ivy.

Mostly though, our bird population is rather common-or-garden, considering our surroundings of field and woodland, here in the middle of nowhere: just the ubiquitous blackbirds, blue tits, chaffinches and doves. Will we eventually end up looking on them as harbingers of disease, like rats? Reports of outbreaks of H5N1 in northern Hungary and Slovenia.

As far as I can understand, in some parts of the world, avian flu is now endemic in the wild bird population at a low level. Species, like waterfowl, that flock together in water are most prone. The disease is passed on to commercial flocks that practise poor bio-security and then, as a result of the conditions in which they're kept, mutates to a more virulent form. This is exactly the sort of environment where it could mutate again into a virus that will infect humans.

8th
Cockcrow 5.30
The earth's axis has tilted to create the new season, but today I feel it's just tipped back again. A quick sortie into the cold, neat kitchen garden yields

a bracing spring tonic – a trugful of early rhubarb, hidden away in its nest of straw under a bamboo cloche.

The main crop is grown in a row at the bottom of the garden, like a huge hedge, with spikey 6ft flowers. Concerned visitors tell me, I should stop them flowering – it detracts from the plants' vigour. I long for something to weaken them before they take over the whole plot: I divide the plants for sale into pots each year, we urge customers to pick their own, which they do, disappearing home under huge bunches. But still the umbrella leafed trifid thrives.

I first spotted this variety in a garden down the lane. When the owner died and his garden was developed by the local farmer, I asked his builder if he would save a root for me. The next day it arrived filling the entire bucket of a digger. Famed throughout the area, it is now known as rhubarb variety 'Mr Batchelor' after my sadly deceased neighbour.

The plants like a damp spot, with plenty of space to spread their huge leaves, and need eating soon after they've been picked before they go soft and flaccid. Early stalks are sweeter than those picked later in the season, just right for a rhubarb fool.

Cut 1lb/450g rhubarb into chunks. Pop in a pan with ¼ lb/120g sugar and a large knob of butter. Add the grated rind of half an orange and a little chopped preserved ginger. Cover and cook on a very low heat for about eight minutes till soft. Mash with a wooden spoon.

Blend with crème fraîche or whipped double cream, adding more sugar if necessary. Chill in pretty bowls and serve topped with pared orange

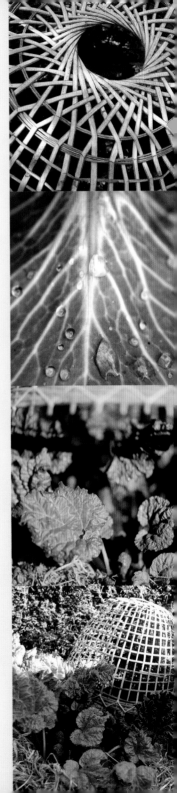

rind. For a change, try a couple of stalks of angelica chopped and cooked with the rhubarb, instead of ginger and orange and chef Sally Clarke suggests a lovely pudding of baked rhubarb, served on meringue with blood orange segments.

My own favourite is a rhubarb crumble topped with equal parts of porridge oats, crushed walnuts and muscovado sugar, moistened with walnut oil and browned in a hot oven.

Forced rhubarb from the Wakefield triangle has been available from the shops since the outset of the year, but I like to wait for my own, it has a deeper flavour.

Used in the 13th century as a laxative, this spectacular looking plant is actually a vegetable, and in the past, thrifty housewives often eked out their precious strawberry jam with rhubarb stalks. Rhubarb sauce is suggested as an apt accompaniment to oily fish, and so is sorrel.

Pick a large pan of tender young sorrel leaves, sweat them in butter with a couple of leeks, and dilute for soup with a pintful of vegetable stock. Liquidize and season with salt, black pepper and grated nutmeg and swirl with a spoonful of crème fraîche. Try and eat it all up before the sorrel looses its lively green colour.

A creamy sorrel purée makes a tasty nest for a freshly poached egg, or a delicious sauce poured over a plate of halved, soft boiled eggs.

Sorrel grows like a weed, best in a damp spot, and quick to sprout in the early days of spring, when its welcome acid bite livens the palate after a winter of stodgy roots. I grow buckler-leaved sorrel in the salad beds, where it self-seeds happily and adds a little lemony flavour to spring leaves. Try it with finely chopped young nettles and watercress or as a topping for a toasted cream cheese sandwich.

10th

The moorhens have taken to travelling around the garden on the tops of the yew and lonicera hedges. Their huge feet, adapted to walking on lily pads and marshy ground, make this an easy feat. Keeps them safe from the cat, who knows the hens and ducks are family, but enjoys a nice moorhen or two. Thank heavens she's getting older, and her kills are mercifully fewer. I urge the moorhens to remember they are not flightless, they could always fly away.

14th

Make contact with Chris Ashton from the British Call Duck Club. She seems very abreast of the H5N1 situation, *au fait* with the scientific aspects and ready to do battle. Suggest we fight side by side. So we join together with the British Waterfowl, Call Duck and Indian Runner Duck Associations, the Goose and Turkey Clubs, the Poultry Club of Great Britain, the Araucana Club and the Scots Dumpy Club in a joint effort to persuade Defra to allow us to vaccinate our birds.

A quick lunch for a cousin from Strasbourg, paying a flying visit. Mix a carton of Greek yoghurt with a small clove of crushed garlic and season with salt. Divide into two bowls.

Simmer a frying pan of water and carefully shell and drop in four eggs, one in each corner. Poach for three minutes or until cooked to your taste. Remove with a slotted spoon and leave to drain on a piece of kitchen paper. Fry a knob of butter with a few sprigs of mint and a little paprika till brown, add a quick squeeze of lemon – be careful, it will splutter. Pop the eggs on a bed of yoghurt and drizzle the hot butter sauce over the eggs. Serve with French bread – my guest will eat nothing else – and a little creamed spinach.

An easy English pud: a pretty pink rhubarb jelly.
Cut 1lb/450g of rhubarb into tiny chunks, and place in a pan with 4oz/120g sugar and ¼ pt/150ml of water. Simmer till soft and strain, squashing the pulp with a wooden spoon to extract all the juice.

Meanwhile put 3 tablespoons of very hot water in a bowl and sprinkle in ½ sachet of gelatine. Leave for a few minutes, then stir till dissolved. Take a half pint/300ml measuring jar and fill with rhubarb juice, adding water to make up the measure. Add a dash of Vin d'Orange, or Cointreau, and mix in the jelly. Leave to set in the fridge. For a really exciting bubbly effect, whisk the jelly again just before it sets, then pour into special champagne flutes and set again in the fridge.

15th

The warmer weather heralds the extinguishing of the Rayburn. Unless the temperature drops dramatically again, it will stay turned off until next autumn, so any cooking from now on has to be done on the electric hob, or in our small oven and grill. Could be a false spring, with false hopes and fragrant, warm soft days. There's a buzz in the air urging me to clear the garden – to paint the outdoor furniture, prune the shrubs, and cut back the perennials. But I always leave at least six inches of old spiky growth to protect young shoots from pecking beaks, webbed feet and gobbling bills.

Divide my beloved artichoke plants, with the bread knife, (don't tell Max, he has a horror of kitchen, garden and hens overlapping, insisting on a stringent hygiene regime, maybe he should consider a career with Health and Safety) and pop the slips in six inch pots of compost, for sale in the yard when they have rooted.

Hurrah. Max has finished the beach buggy that he has been building single-handed from scratch in the garage over the past few years. Am so proud, it passes its MOT at first attempt. Go for a celebratory drive with him. My head nearly falls off and my ears are still ringing. Let's hope his characteristic creativity and tenaciousness are rewarded soon with a full-time job, instead of endless, unpaid work experience.

16th

Heavy late frosts. Pray my walnut, quince and apricot crop isn't ruined. Am convinced our obsession with the weather stems from the fact it is so unpredictable. In early March the temperature fell below freezing, a few weeks later you could eat a meal sitting outside in the sun, and now we are shivering again.

Report out from Newcastle University on the devastation caused by Foot and Mouth five years ago. It cost 1.3 billion in compensation, culling and clean up costs. Other businesses, the farm suppliers and tourist economy lost 39 million. The farmers, with their strong traditional parliamentary support and their effective union were well compensated, the others were not. Defra was created as a result; let's hope they succeed where their predecessors failed.

To Northumberland myself, to a friend Jane Torday's establishment - the Garden Station, to give a hen keeping course with a guest spot for my co-star, a canny breeder with a passion for black and white bantams. A most beautiful landscape so different from our flat, wide skies. Jane's ancient farmhouse looks out immediately on a russet coloured hill crossed with sheep tracks, a landscape that fills the entire vista.

18th

Spring cleaning in the chicken run, in anticipation of a visit from Chris Graham, the editor of Practical Poultry magazine, coming to interview and photograph me and the girls for an article. Conscientiously, I sweep under the verandah, where the feeders and drinkers are kept. I clean out the metal-lidded galvanized dustbin that stores the mixed corn, away from the depredations of other less welcome diners, and sort all the hen keeping paraphernalia

– the old dustpan with a sturdy hand brush hanging next to the wallpaper scraper, perfect for the removal of any stubborn bits when cleaning out the houses. I fastidiously tidy the straw for the nest boxes, the pile of newspapers to line their sleeping quarters, and the bottles of disinfectant, the rubber gloves, and the old washing up brush to scour the drinkers.

Great efforts to make sure the run measures up to Defra's guidelines, and although I have managed to feed the ducks and hens separately for the last month or so, a pair of ducks somehow manage to appear in almost every shot.

26th

To Assington Mill to give a hen keeping course. The energy of its recently retired owners is exhausting. This is an amazing venture, to convert a truly derelict watermill, outhouses and barns plus eighty acres, into a home, educational centre and organically self sustaining farm. The lectures are held in a straw bale barn, warm and snug. There is even a course on straw bale building, which I'm hoping a friend of mine will attend, because I hanker after a straw bale wall to keep my veggie garden sheltered and protected.

The appetite of the British middle-aged lady for knowledge on these courses, is as inspiring as their hosts' ingenuity to supply. At an age, where many would have been donning slippers or just pottering, others are performing Herculean tasks and fulfilling long-held ambitions. I find talking on these occasions pretty exhausting and afterwards the longing to potter looms large. But it's always fascinating to meet those with similar interests, and gives me the chance to get the subject off my chest, thus delivering family and friends from my passions.

Despite our worries, most places on our own courses, Counting your Chickens and Knowing your Onions are taken up.

28th

4.30pm, give an interview on Radio Scotland. The Henkeepers' Association sends a letter of support to the Dutch Poultry Club, who is lobbying their Minister today for vaccination. Receive an email from Alma:

"All keepers of hens and waterfowl feel thoroughly bad to lock up their birds, and so do I. It breaks my heart to see their area restricted. The object is to keep them in a pen with a roof over their head, that doesn't allow droppings of wild birds to go through. The covering sheets of plastic are getting weighed down again with snow, and the construction could collapse at any time. The gardener is coming in again to fix it. Never thought I would come to dread snow.

Next month the vaccine is available, there will be rush on vets and so higher costs, and the vaccination must be repeated three weeks later. We are worried many birds will not survive the stress".

29th

Booked to be the 'sofa' guest by Lesley Dolphin on her morning show on BBC Radio Suffolk next week. Hopefully will get a chance to plug the Hen Party and quell fears.

Lots of worryingly large bills coming in. Receive new legal advice that a limited company is unnecessary, so with relief write to Companies House to dissolve Henkeepers' Association Ltd. What a waste of money. Am considering putting the website on-line free of charge, because I now realize the point of the internet culture – to encourage the free flow of information, and I'm keen to prove to Defra the true level of support for vaccination.

Evan, our local ace carpenter delivers a new batch of henhouses. Like a multi-coloured row of tiny Southwold beach huts, some with runs for night-time safety, or space for broodies and chicks.

30th

Pick up plants from Martin's Nursery at Bradfield St George. Finally all the threads for the hen party have woven to form a jolly spring patchwork: the marquee, tables, breeders, and helpers have all been booked, organized and alerted. The cakes, different coloured eggs in baskets and Easter goodies are ordered. The stock is all in place. Optimism at this time of the year is always tempered with residual worry about the weather. All previous six hen parties have taken place in sub arctic temperatures, presided over by a hypothermic organizer with a red nose, jabbering incoherently, shivering with cold, and unable to grasp the entrance money with frozen fingers.

31st

Decide, with regret, that due to the pall hanging over us all, after discussions with the breeders who normally show, and in order to avoid red tape and keep safe, it would be better not to exhibit any birds at the Hen Party this year. The show ban has been lifted nationally, but the disease restrictions and precautions would be untenable for a small set-up like this. So a press release goes out and is taken up by all the local papers, who manage to use it as further ammunition to fan the flames of frenzy about the disease.

Pray that our customers will support us anyway, but I'm not sure they've all been contacted. Earlier in the year, a friend in the village, whose secretary has meticulously compiled my databases for the last ten years, announced that they had worryingly been burgled. Their office computers had been stolen. And all my mailing lists: 1500 shop customers, over 10,000 mail order book customers and address book of suppliers had been lost because the data had never been saved.

I'm still angry and miserable, because, inevitably we fell out as a result. So now the invitation mailing list has been posted for the Hen Party and other forthcoming attractions, without those invaluable keen new customers whose addresses we gleaned last year. To add insult to injury, we'll have to contend with the public's continued unfounded fears of catching bird flu from any passing chicken, and that all birds should be avoided at all costs. But I think in the end, less customers will come, simply because there will be no lovely hens to look at.

They'll miss stalwarts like Hugh's prize-winning Silkie hen - Showgirl, Sally Hutton will be there without her tiny

Barbu D'Uccle cockerel perched on her shoulder, and Pauline will come, but her broodies and their chicks will have to stay at home. Colin and Paul will just bring photos of their gigantic Cochins and Mike Faiers will have Brahma hatching eggs only for sale. (Fertile eggs are available from most breeders at this time of the year, so hen keepers can augment their flocks with any breed under the sun, by popping a few eggs under broodies and hatching to order).

We were hoping Chris Reeves would show his rare Ixworths, that the Kneens would bring their blue and black Orpingtons, and that Carol from Stableyard Poultry would show her Dutch bantams. In previous years, breeders like Janice Houghton-Wallace have stolen the show with outstanding turkeys, the duck man has charmed us with lavender Runners, and Liz has amazed us with Araucana hens that lay pretty blue eggs. This year, we'll all just have to make do.

APRIL

1st

The dawn chorus wakes me: the crowing, cooing, chirruping, quacking and twittering builds to a deafening crescendo. I must admit, to my shame, being really irritated at times by the free-form modern jazz notes of the songthrush. I agree with Shakespeare: "the sweet birds, O how they sing! Doth set my pugging tooth on edge".

2nd

Everyone is nesting. The patient moorhen builds her nest and lays the first of her clutches on the pontoon. The black and white duck, the only duck I lay claim to, has settled in the nettle bed near the pond. I could take her eggs to eat, but you have to be quick off the mark. Duck eggs have a rich flavour and need to be eaten very fresh. The shell is more porous than a hen's eggshell, and their shelf life is a mere 8 days.

For a soft boiled duck's egg, simmer for 5 minutes and then allow to rest for a further five. Duck eggs are low in the foam producing protein globulin and can't be whisked, so save them for rich scrambled eggs and custards.

En masse, my flock has gone broody and I try to keep an eye on all my ladies. They are thankfully predictable in their nesting places – always in one or other of the henhouses – we have several in our chicken village. Not so next door's bantams, who prefer the compost heaps and hedgerows, occasionally building nests in the churchyard. Luckily the handsome Cockerel doesn't fancy these tiny birds, or we'd be overrun with weird and wonderful crossbreeds. But the youngest Orpington *is* laying away. I can tell by the purposeful way she struts down the garden path, but I can't find her nest.

So I shadow her, sneakily. Laying hens are very wise to observers and will casually occupy themselves with all sorts of sophistry, waiting for the minute you lose concentration. Finally, from a hiding place behind a bush – have I gone mad? – I watch her march up to a sitting duck nesting on the compost heap, peck her hard on the head till she moves over and then settle in her place to lay an egg - one of eighteen – a dozen blue and the rest her own, pretty and tinted beige. As the sly hussy leaves, the victimized duck takes over. I'm afraid I took all the eggs away in the end. My menagerie is diverse enough, without a troupe of hens who think they're ducks and vice versa.

Most pure breeds go broody and want to hatch their eggs, some are more prone than others. Traditionally, Silkies and their crossbreeds are the most successful mums, but it's easier to list the popular breeds that don't sit: Anconas, Bresse, Hamburghs, Leghorns, Minorcas, Polands, Scots Greys and Welsummers (though there are the odd exceptions).

If you keep a cockerel and allow your flock a relatively natural existence, they will start to behave in pre-domesticated way. Each hen will lay a clutch of eggs (probably between 8 and 10) and even though you are removing them for the kitchen, she will go broody. Outwardly aggressive to interference and fluffed up beyond recognition, left to her own devices, she will sit on these eggs for 21 days till they hatch. If you don't want chicks, you may be able to divert her at an early stage by removing

any eggs, closing the nestbox or destroying her nest, and then taking her to the other end of the garden to show her something amazing that she really likes – an ant's nest maybe, or a cabbage or the avian equivalent to Johnny Depp. You may distract your broody, but otherwise she's there for the duration – three weeks.

I often just let them stay and have a three week holiday, taking away the eggs and making sure they eat, drink and perform their toilette. But being broody puts a strain on their health. Their temperature is artificially raised. Hormonally charged, they go on a diet, fall prey to parasites and don't get enough exercise. So, once a year is enough.

4th

Spring cleaning. I'm not really a housewifely sort of person, but as the sap rises, the genes of my grandmother (who lived in a self-imposed howling draught all her life) come to the fore. I can move mountains in this sort of mood. My family has learnt over the years to make themselves scarce, best not to get in the way or they may have to help. Windows are flung open and I get the urge to clean, to invite the fresh smells of spring into the house. My friend, Penelope Hands, gives a recipe for beeswax polish perfumed with lavender oil or crushed sweet cicely seeds, in her book, *Beekeeping for Beginners*.

Put 8oz/250g beeswax and 1½pints/850ml of real turpentine in an old catering size tin, and leave to stand in a pan of

85

boiling water till the wax melts. Boil 1½ pints/850ml distilled water with 3 tsp. soapflakes, 3 tsp. washing soda and ½ tsp. ammonia in an old saucepan, and add to the melted wax mixture with a few drops of lavender oil, beating with a rotary whisk for 10 minutes – good for the arm muscles. Pour the cooled polish into five honey jars and leave to cool. Pop on the lids and label.

5th

I usually start sorting my seeds now, I don't actually sow many till the beginning of May, the temperature here can still fluctuate wildly. But I like to get the new packets of seeds out and plan. Broad beans get snugly interred, maybe a row of wild rocket in the unusually tidy vegetable garden, the rest wait. Most will be planted at the end of the month in pots in the conservatory, that way you hedge your bets, and the rotation of crops and design of your potager can be more carefully plotted.

6th

A Mute Swan has been found in Scotland and is suspected of having died of avian influenza. Lots of calls from the media, including one from the Today Programme. I wait a nail-biting two hours to hear whether I'm being interviewed. Mercifully I'm not. The third degree from John Humphreys would be the last straw. Perhaps I'm being paranoid, but I get the feeling that some of the media think we are a non-essential whimsy and because we don't keep our hens in the same totally biosecure surroundings as the industry – in batteries – we are endangering our communities.

It is the mobile wild birds that link and pass on the disease to commercial flocks, not our static domestic poultry. There is, please God, little evidence to prove the mutation from bird to human will take place in this country. And eventually the spread of the disease between humans will be as a result of our own mobility, as proved by the SARS virus.

7th

Woke at 5am, hearing the Cockerel's strange muted cry, and remembered with a sinking heart, that tests on the badly decomposed body of the swan discovered at Cellardyke in Fife have proved positive. It is a Whooper swan, not native to these shores, and tests on other wild birds are proving negative. Turned on the news to wait with bated breath. Birds within a 3km zone are to be kept undercover.

Word from Toddy Hamilton-Guild, Secretary of the Scots Dumpy Club and keen supporter of vaccination, is that one of the most significant flocks of Dumpies is within the 10km restriction zone, and must not be moved. Scots Dumpies are a rare breed in need of urgent conservation. Must get up and update the Henkeepers' Association website. At least, we haven't all been forced to keep our birds undercover as a precaution, like they have in Germany and Holland. Thank you, Ben Bradshaw for small mercies.

8th

Lots of eggs. Time to bake a Simnel cake and make the marzipan to top it off:

Cream together 6oz/175g butter, 4oz/120g caster sugar and a large spoonful of honey. Beat in three large eggs and fold in 8oz/250g plain flour with a tsp. of baking powder. Add 4oz/120g each of currants, dates and raisins, plus the pared rind of a lemon. Mix well and turn into an 8 inch tin, lined with greaseproof paper. Bake for 1½ hrs at 375F/190C, checking every now and again while you make the marzipan.

Take equal amounts of sugar and ground almonds and bind them together with beaten egg and a squeeze of lemon juice. Mix, knead and roll out, sprinkling icing sugar on your board to stop it sticking. Roll up 11 small balls (said to represent the 11 apostles) and put aside to decorate the cake, plus a nugget (presumably Judas) to hide inside the cake before cooking, using the rest to cover the top with a thick layer. Pop the whole cake under the grill to brown.

A quick lunch.

Take a wholemeal roll. Cut off the top and hollow out the inside – the hens will enjoy the crumbs. Crack a nice fresh egg inside, cover with mushrooms and gruyère cheese. Pop in a hot oven for about 10 minutes until the white of the egg is set. Replace the top. Take out to the garden to eat in the pale spring sunshine.

Back in to scour the newspapers for news for the website, come across a moving piece in The Guardian by poet John Burnside, writing from the afflicted area in Scotland, regretting the loss of birds from sight, and concluding that we mustn't "sacrifice what communication we have left with the few birds we still know, for the sake of visibly adequate, but possibly cosmetic response".

88

CHICORY   CHERVIL

11th

The Beauty has gone broody. She is my loveliest hen, a two year old. I'd like to hatch a couple of new pullets to keep us in eggs for the next few years. I have a system: every year I replace the old ladies who drop off one end of the perch with one or two hatchlings who will lay and promote the line. So, this is a broody I want to encourage.

13th

Having waited to see if she is seriously fluffed up, cross and broody, I place two of her own eggs under her, after dark, holding them under my gloved hand to protect them from pecks. Once she has settled, I move her to a special broody house with its own run, give her a quick spray with anti-parasite spray and shut her in till she's used to her change of address. As a new mum and inexperienced brooder, I take her out every other day and make sure she eats, drinks and performs her toilette – the old hands will do this without your help or supervision.

Twenty one days from the day your broody started sitting on the eggs (NOT the day the eggs were laid) the chicks will hatch. Maybe a couple of days before, you might hear cheeping inside the nest. It's the chicks chatting to their mum inside the egg. Don't get involved helping the hatch. I believe that a chick that is strong enough to survive will have the energy to extricate itself on its own without help. Leave the new family for two days, and mum will lead her brood out. Clean out the nest and take away any eggs that haven't hatched. Your role is supervisory.

Americans like white eggs to eat – they believe them to be cleaner. We prefer brown eggs, thinking them healthier. But all eggs, be they brown, white, tinted or blue, are the same under the shell. Most Mediterranean breeds – Leghorns, Minorcas, or Anconas lay white eggs; Marans, Welsummers and Croad Langshans lay rich brown eggs, and South American birds lay bluish green, the rest lay a nice tinted beige egg.

The colour of the yolk is determined in nature by the amount of greenery the bird consumes, and in the commercial industry by additives to feed. Their latest trick is to add marigold petals that result in unnaturally lurid technicolour orange yolks, somehow even more of a travesty than the usual pale yellow blobs that stare up at you from the bowl from shop bought eggs.

15th
Easter Saturday

THE HEN PARTY
(Gentlemen welcome)
Herald the new season, with Amateur Breeders and Fanciers,
Showing their hens, ducks, turkeys and peacocks for sale and to order.
Pure breed eggs for hatching.
Simnel cakes, lemon curd, meringues, jams and honey.
Organic free range eggs. Vegetable, herb and perennial plants.
See the Amazing Eglu Henhouse and the Incredible Insect Circus.
Egg hunt for children in the Churchyard.
Delicious refreshments served in St Mary's Church.
Giant Chocolate Easter Egg
Raffle to raise money for Repairs.
Entrance £1.00
(includes a chocolate egg for each child).

This invitation went out to what's left of my mailing list. Last year, a bitterly cold easterly wind didn't deter the 1500 visitors who overwhelmed us with their enthusiasm and numbers. The Church raised a gratifying sum. It was a cheery start to the season. Today, the pall of the media hype about bird flu hangs over us and attendance is down to 400. The marquee on the lawn is full of breeders, but without their usual birds, all decked out in their spring plumage. We would have had to get special permission, have a vet in attendance, probably provide a disinfectant footbath for customers, it's all too depressing. But strangely enough, despite everything, it is a pleasant day, and good weather for a change. Those who come - the hardcore, are determined to enjoy themselves. With plenty of space, everyone relaxes and the new season is duly christened.

If there was ever a recipe that conjured up Easter, using up both yolk and white of egg, this is it - a Lemon Meringue Ice Cream from Penny Hands that uses homemade meringue and lemon curd. I love lemon curd: a sublimely unctuous concoction with just the right balance of sweet and sharpness.

To make more than enough for the ice cream, beat two large whole eggs plus two extra yolks in a jug. Put 4oz/120g cubed unsalted butter, 4oz/120g sugar and the grated rind and juice of two large lemons in a basin. Pour the eggs in through a sieve, and put the basin over a saucepan of simmering water and cook, stirring regularly, until the curd thickens. Cool and spoon into sterilized jars.

Whisk the two leftover egg whites till they form stiff peaks, slowly adding 4oz/120g caster sugar. Spoon the mixture in blobs onto a grease-proofed tray and pop in a medium oven (350F/170C) for 20 minutes. Cool on a wire rack.

Penny's really easy ice cream combines these confections with double cream. Fold a small jar of lemon curd into a 500ml pot of double cream, add 3 or 4 crumbled meringues and a little lemon juice. Freeze to serve as ice cream. During colder months, this mixture unfrozen makes a refreshing moussey pud, served in pretty glasses with a little lemon or lime zest, pared on top.

16th

Letter from Ben Bradshaw, repeating the government's view on the limitations of vaccination, but informing us that the Henkeepers' Association is to be put on the Stakeholders' Database. Reply from the Prince of Wales's private secretary to our letter, asking for support. His Royal Highness was interested to read our letter, not least because this is a subject in which he takes a particular interest. He admitted he could well understand our anxieties about the threat which avian flu poses to pure and traditional breeds of poultry. The letter went on to suggest we contact Patrick Holden of the Soil Association.

20th

Am woken at 5.13am by the persistent quack of a mother duck calling her young. It's the drain again. I go out in the mist with a long handled sieve, lift the heavy drain cover in the lane, and fish out the ducklings that have fallen in between the bars. Am attacked by the duck. She races off with her family. I find a piece of netting to put under the drain grill. Every year, there is one day when all the mother

The
KITCHEN
GARDEN

2 pints

HEN

HENS

Keyrings £2·50
Labels £1·00
Pack of
labels £5·00
Hanging
Signs £4·50

Plain slate can be
marked with
white felt tip

DUCKS
IN YOUR GARDEN

GOOSE
ON THE GREEN

HENS
IN YOUR GARDEN

EGGS
EGGS
EGGS
EGGS
EGGS

ducks appear with their mega broods on cue. There must have been a moment, 28 days ago when there was a massive duck sex fest. I watch their vulnerable beginnings with a heavy heart. I'd love to cherish all these little comics, but they are wild birds.

Unable to get back to sleep, I head off early into the vegetable garden. How neat and tidy it all looks at this time of the year, before everything starts growing huge and out of control. Just as well. Tomorrow we open the shop and garden for the first of our regular Friday and Saturday open days, and everything has to look pretty. It's easy to do in the spring, but later in the year, it can be an overwhelming task, unless I remind myself to keep it real. The hens aren't helping. They are obsessed with the compost heaps, a good sign they have rotted down sufficiently to be dismantled and spread on to the beds before planting out begins next month.

21st

First cuckoo – usually such a joyous moment, but not this year. Maybe she is bringing the dreaded virus with her from Africa via Europe. Surely not, how could a bird with a deadly disease fly that far? Those other smaller harbingers of spring, the scout ants, are optimistically scurrying over the tiles towards the larder. I use defiantly non ecological methods to deter them before they bring in their millions of mates. Cheer myself with a small bunch of vulnerable spring flowers, to put on the kitchen table, where visitors have their coffee and cakes.

The shop is full of stock, overstocked in fact, because of fewer customers to the Hen Party. I put out all the garden goodies: generous Italian seed packets; huge reels of tarry smelling string from Scotland; glamorous leather aprons and pouches from Cumbria; the best gardening gloves in the world – strong enough to prune roses, but light enough for delicate seedlings; potter Rob Wheeler's terracotta pots; Danish enamelled watering cans, galvanized buckets, brushes, slate markers, and the odd antique, all to one side of the tiny brick shed.

At the other end goes all the hen keeping paraphernalia: the galvanized corn scoops, drinkers and feeders, the china broody eggs in four sizes, the wicker carriers, pills and potions, Rob's bantam egg cups, wooden trays - hand painted by Kate and Hannah Breach with colourful pure breeds, and every type of egg container known to man – egg boxes, egg trays and egg racks. The books, cards and jam pots are kept in the house, to keep the damp from curling covers and labels.

Outside in the yard you'll find vegetable seedlings, flower and fruit plants, cloches, containers and pots, plants supports and painted henhouses. I try and find makers and suppliers who are local and unusual, and to obey William Morris's edict that all my products should be known to be useful or believed to be beautiful. A tall order in a retail world of cheap, mass produced and omnipresent tat, but I love playing shop and setting out my wares.

22nd

Flying visit to the farmer's market for treats, before opening again to a busy day. Thank heavens for the hellebores, still flowering their socks off and the inevitable euphorbias, because apart from the blossom, there is little colour in the garden for visitors to see. The hens look magnificent though, decked in their mating plumage, a real tonic to see that wonderful uplifting soft apricot colour in blobs around the garden. I'm often asked why I love the Orpingtons so, when there are so many amazing breeds to choose from, many of whom could do with the extra fillip of a little celebrity endorsement. Ultimately it's their friendliness I love, and being extremely short-sighted, it would be pointless to have something small, rare and subtle, lurking unseen at the bottom of the garden.

One of the most determinedly rare breeds in need of help is the Ixworth. Our nearest large village is called Ixworth. Does it, like Orpington have a chicken named after it? About ten years ago, while researching old books, I came across a faint picture of an Ixworth and decided to investigate. According to locals, it was extinct, but a letter to the excellent Rare Poultry Society confirmed that although not common, there were a few flocks, including a small collection owned by a breeder near Cambridge.

We visited in early May. Alas, the Ixworth is not a pretty bird. White feathered, with greyish legs, a small pea comb, and an angular heavy body, we felt nonetheless that it should be brought back to its birthplace and took three fertile eggs to be brooded successfully under a friend's hen in Ixworth.

The Ixworth was invented by the late Mr Appleyard at Priory Waterfowl Farm to fulfil demands for layer/table birds just after the Second World War, when the government was striving for self-sufficiency and battery farming was in its infancy. Possibly nowadays it would not have merited pure breed status, just a hybrid patent. A medal-winning cross between

White Sussex, Orpington, Minorca, English and Indian Game birds, there is a fondly remembered resemblance between Mr Appleyard and his creation among the old boys in the village.

Recently, I heard that a pure breed specialist was developing the Ixworth in great numbers in the hope of producing the British equivalent of Poulet de Bresse. – a table bird *par excellence. Bonne chance.* Will producers over here adhere to statutory regulations that the French lay down as obligatory to rear their famous roast chicken? 10 square metres of free ranging per bird, with requisite greenery, specific feed: wheat, maize and milk, plus whatever they can forage; to be slaughtered at 16 weeks as opposed to a lifespan in this country of 6 to 8 weeks (rising to 10 for organic free range); and most of all, will the British Housewife pay? I gather they do get some takers at Harrods Food Hall for Poulet de Bresse at £25.00 a bird.

We have choices: chicken becomes more economical if the whole carcass is cooked. Every time we eat breast alone, the bits and feet wing their way by the containerful to China – the producer is exporting all the thrift and creativity we should be using in the kitchen. We should celebrate, by making top grade chicken a special occasion dish, not part of a three times a day protein habit. We all eat too much animal protein. I've long since given up chicken meat. It's either the product of a system I abhor, or a creature I know too well.

26th

About 30 years ago an old school friend, Jane gave me a wondrous fern from her garden at Sancreed in Cornwall. It still flourishes in a huge pot, benefiting from the rain that sheets down from the unguttered shop roof. Along with it came a hidden present: some tiny three cornered leaf wild garlic bulbs which have blessedly naturalized themselves in various spots.

I wonder how many of the garden's treasures have appeared uninvited, hitching a lift in a potted present? I never actually planted the Campanula *portenschlagiana* (which ought to be ashamed of a name like that) or the huge Silybum marianum - Our Lady's milkweed thistles, or the ubiquitous Shoo-fly plant, all more than flourishing and sometimes overwhelming their host. They may be invasive, but occasionally, like the garlic, they are welcome guests. I often bless these pretty white bluebell flowers and garlic flavoured leaves in early spring, livening up a broth or adding zest to springtime salads - a flavour more delicate than its pungent Ransons or field garlic cousins.

This is a rather old fashioned supper dish that turns the seasonal excess of eggs and garlic into a tasty family meal.

Hard boil half a dozen eggs, (they don't have to be your freshest) shelling them under running cold water, and then halving and placing them sunny side up in a buttered ovenproof dish. Make a white sauce by melting an ounce of butter in a saucepan, mixing in a tablespoon of flour and then stirring carefully while diluting with ½ pint/300ml of milk. Pour the sauce over the eggs.

Wilt a handful of wild garlic (or leeks or spring onions) in a little butter and arrange on top of the dish. Cover with grated cheese and bake for 10 minutes in a hot oven until brown and crispy on top. Garnish with chopped wild garlic or parsley.

MAY

Seedlings

Asparagus

Lilac Flowers

Apple Blossom

Sowing Salads

Peas and Beans

Chicks Hatching

1st

Three Norfolk farms, not far from here, have been infected with H5N7, a mercifully low pathenogenic strain of avian flu, posing little threat to humans or other birds. A one kilometre restriction zone has been set up, but local hen keepers are not being asked to house their pets. East Anglia is home to the largest concentration of poultry flocks in Europe. Many of these birds start life as chicks hatched in France, which are then transported to Britain as day olds, spend their early growing days in one unit and then are sent off to their farms at point of lay. Their laying days over, after just two years, these hapless creatures are then driven away to be dispatched. Their much travelled carcasses tot up as many road and airmiles in their short and pathetic lives as any seasoned globetrotter, ending up finally as petfood. Plenty of opportunity for spreading disease and yet we're told it's wild birds that spread avian influenza. Are they the vectors or the victims?

3rd

Three of my mate Fred's precious Hamburghs have died suddenly. He lives within 10 miles of the outbreak and has tried so hard to improve and increase his flock, with little help from their breed club. He has had to contact the authorities, despite misgivings that it might result in a visit from the men in white. Relief to hear later that the deaths had been caused by rat poison. Sad, but not as sad as it might have been. We've all been overrun with vermin this year.

4th

On a cheerier note, my Beauty has hatched two chicks. With her looks and their dad's stamina, they will be stunners. If I were a breeder, I'd concentrate on her offspring, discarding all others, but like most of us,

I have a penchant for the underdog, for the also ran, and I'm far too disorganized. They tell me Beauty is show standard, but that would mean keeping her out of the sun - to protect her colour, away from the rest of the flock - to preserve her plumage. I know I don't have that sort of steely determination.

Leafing through a poultry magazine, I come across a pertinent article – 'Raise your Chicks the Natural Way' – meaning under a broody as opposed to in an incubator. I was horrified to see photos of the mums imprisoned behind bars in slatted cages, through which the chicks could come and go, but the mum had to stay put, unable to protect her babes. I know we're exceptionally lucky not to have a wide range of predators here, but even if you have to cage your hens and chicks, at least keep them together in a mobile run. There is a mean streak in many traditional poultry habits. Do these breeders actually like their birds?

Books, mostly by breeders, imply that cocks and other members of the flock are a danger to chicks, but for the last five years, I've kept my young ones caged only for their first few days, then let them into the main run (after the adult occupants have left for the morning). Mums have taken their small broods out into the great unknown of the garden to run with the flock, at their own discretion – usually at about a week old.

Stately as galleons my big hens sail majestically across the lawn, sedately picking their way around their offspring, keenly examining the garden for danger or minutely examining the ground for delicacies to pass on to their babes. These fluffy eggs on legs, hop and skitter, safe in the knowledge that their mum will shelter and defend them. Sticking to the hedges and garden edges for shelter, so far, we've had no disasters. Mothers teach their chicks valuable lessons – brooded birds are much more streetwise than their incubated cousins, but obviously you have to be around to supervise. Danger can come from overhead; from raptors and magpies; during the night from hedgehogs, rats and foxes, and by day from mink, squirrels, cats and dogs.

Despite the broodies, there are still plenty of eggs.

Clafoutis is an eggy Mediterranean pancake dish of seasonal fruit with a vanilla flavoured 4 egg batter poured over it. Then it's baked quickly under a grill till set and sprinkled with caster sugar. I like to add 7oz/200g of ricotta cheese to the batter and fry one side, grilling the other, to avoid any clever dick pancake turning.

If it hasn't turned tough yet, you could use rhubarb, poached with a few angelica stems, but later in the season why not try gooseberries, cherries, as they do in France, or my favourite – apricots? You can make a savoury version by adding a purée of any cooked vegetable to the basic batter. Baked aubergine with basil, fried courgettes with rosemary, or blanched chard with a good squeeze of lemon are all tasty.

5th

The ducklings are not so lucky, they are at the bottom of the food chain and fall prey to everyone, presumably the reason they're produced in such huge numbers – families of 18 are not uncommon. Interminable drake wars upset the balance of broods. Their piping calls stretch my nerves to breaking point, and the tension stops me breathing properly, I'm so busy listening intently for signs of real distress and ready to rush out into the garden like Superwoman to protect my birds. Good mums are balm to the soul, patrolling with their babes in organized waves, fanning out across the lawn to lurch and catch the midges, like a platoon of bumble bees. But they don't stand their ground like the Orpington matrons. They fly off with new suitors and their babies scatter. I don't keep count any more, it's too distressing.

The ducks secretly share their pond with a stealthy collection of moorhens. I never know who's who. And since they are extremely territorial, it seems unlikely more than one pair are in residence, but there is much fighting, calling and chasing. The dominant female has laid her usual clutch in her usual nest at the end of the pontoon. Every time a visitor passes, she leaves and hides, returning the minute they pass. This is the tenth generations of moorhens that have laid on the pontoon, so despite the interruptions to the brooding process, this is obviously a prime site.

6th

London friends to lunch. So want to show off my hens' eggs and try this impressive dish by Penny from our book *The Big Book of Garden Hens*. She suggests these soufflés should be served in old fashioned shallow soup plates, but that we should check that all four plates will fit in the oven before we start.

Pre-heat your oven to 400F/200C. Butter four ovenproof soup plates and sprinkle with a little parmesan. Whisk 4 egg yolks with 4oz/125g soft goats' cheese, and stir in 2 tablespoons crème fraîche. Add 4oz/125g of cooked chopped spinach, some chopped chervil, tarragon or parsley and a good grating of parmesan. Season well.

In a separate bowl, whisk 4 egg whites till stiff and fold into the yolky mixture. Spoon into the plates, add more parmesan and bake for 8-10 minutes. They should look quite moist, because they go on cooking in the plates for a while. Serve immediately, but be careful – the plates will be hot.

The soufflés were eaten with French bread, green salad with a few shredded sorrel leaves and murmurs of appreciation.

8th

To the Essex borders, with a car full of stock, taking a stall as shopping relief for the Gardens Trust annual lunch and lecture. This year we hear the Duchess of Northumberland's saga of her battle to set up a Vegas-style pleasure garden at Alnwick castle, obviously a huge economic success for the region. In olden days, her social position would have allowed her to flood whole valleys and raze whole villages merely to improve a vista. Nowadays, Her Grace has to do battle with Health and Safety. Good luck to her.

Set out my wares in a marquee on a gracious lawn in front of a stately mansion along with the usual suspects - a group of ladies with small gardening businesses to promote. After luncheon, the Trust's members indulge in a little light shopping. Many keep hens that live very privileged lives, and I'm proud that our products end up in such elegant surroundings! Raced back home past fields of acid yellow oilseed rape. If its oil was actually propelling my car, I'd be prepared to put up with the headaches and sore throats that the pollen seems to induce each year.

11th

Panting down the lane this morning through clouds of mayflies (there will be much feasting on the duckpond tonight) along a creamy, frothy highway of mayflowers, cow parsley, elderflowers that'll soon be over in a scatter of petals. The lane is edged with cowslips, making a welcome comeback on verges in this part of the country. When my kids were young, we always came back from a walk with posies of wildflowers. Nowadays, I would feel uncomfortable picking them, just as my egg-collecting father must have felt later in his life. We are all victims of rural political correctness, though of course, in these cases it is perfectly justified.

16th

The apple blossom petals drift like snow across the garden. It's so cold I wouldn't be surprised if it were the real thing. Our tree only fruits every other year. Decades of inefficient pruning have turned this venerable inhabitant of the orchard into a biennial cropper with thousands of tiny fruits of indeterminate variety. The position of this tree, close to the

house, actually influenced the size of our extension when we were converting the original tiny cottage into a family home. We stopped the building short to keep this beauty, virtually the only tree in the original garden. The hens eat the petals, and the abundance of branches encourages me to bring armfuls of budding blossom into the house to flower.

17th

Out early again, staggering along the track through the fields, musing. This track has fourfold usage: the farmer takes his machinery along it to the surrounding fields; the residents of Troston run, walk, and take their dogs to shit (blast them), and the hikers, bikers and riders from far and wide hike, bike and ride. And the original inhabitants, the indigenous wildlife still use these well worn paths, judging by the tracks. The farmers, residents, wildlife and leisure takers, all with conflicting interests in theme park Britain. At the time of writing, round here the farmers are still just ahead in the race for space.

18th

The lilac is flowering. A boring, bushy shrub that proliferates in the gardens of Troston, with garish purple or dirty white panicled flowers that soon rust on the bush, but that smell! There is a list of unremarkable plants, whose perfume specifically evokes the time of the year they flower, or people from the past: hyacinths remind me of post Christmas blues; Daphne *mezereum* of a particular friend; spring narcissi of my aunt; wallflowers conjure up memories of mock GCEs, modest sweet rocket and night scented stock bring back long summer evenings; and the Viburnum *bodnantense* that flowers so valiantly from October through to February reminds me of cold mornings, walking through the frosted garden to feed the ducks. And lilac conjures memories of early picnic lunches eaten on the terrace in the first real sunshine. I pick a huge bunch for the house.

19th

A free day. And it's mild and still. What bliss. Grab my seed box and make for the vegetable plot. Most of our vegetable plants that are sold in the shop are planted by Mary, a better gardener than I, with greenhouse facilities. I manage the easy ones in the conservatory. Both are then transferred to the garden as seedlings at the end of the month. It gives them a better start, less brutal than thinning *in situ*.

I grow salads though in rows, directly into the soil, to cut and come again, shearing the tops of the rows with scissors as the seedlings grow. These plants are never thinned, their proximity one to another encourages them to grow quickly and produce tender saladini. So, in goes another row of spinach, olive leaf rocket, frilly leaved 'Salad Bowl' and 'Bergamo', oak leaved 'Eraclea', orientals Mizuna and Pak Choi, herbs coriander and dill, buckler leaved sorrel and bucks horn 'Erba Stella'. Just a little of each, then I can grow more in succession later on.

Using a stick, I trace a small channel in the tilth, sprinkle in the seed and cover with soil. The area is then promptly cloched or caged. I plant out another row of leeks, from a pot of seedlings on the window sill.

Favourites in the kitchen and easy to grow, leeks are much less susceptible to pests and diseases than onions. This may be one of five or six plantings that I make, pretty much throughout the year. My final task is to prepare a trench for my Borlotti beans 'Lingua di Fuoco' that can either be eaten young like runner beans or later, dried in soups. The secret of my limited success is to line the bottom of the trench with soaked newspaper bedding from the henhouses, a nitrogen-rich *papier-mâché* root run for greedy beans.

I'm an impatient gardener and take too little time preparing and planting. My mind is already racing ahead to harvesting and eating. I once watched gardener Anne Swithenbank performing a simple task for the television cameras, and impressed by her methodical deliberation, I try now to remember to enunciate her name - Anne Swith-en-bank – slowly and carefully as my mantra to calm me as I garden.

Next year I shall get some help here in the kitchen garden. Vegetables need regular attention during the season, and sometimes pressure of work has me elsewhere., usually here at the computer. When I get back out, the weeds have overtaken me and I panic, especially if we're opening the next day to the public. I love working here and so it's not an easy decision to make.

20th

Asparagus. Ah, those first few shoots. We are trying three new varieties of crowns: 'Purple Albenga', 'White Venetian' and wild 'Scaber Montina' from Seeds of Italy, who supply generous packs of superb seeds that have been available in this country now for several years. To encourage yield, we won't be picking from these varieties for the first couple of years.

This green soup will use the sporadic yield from my old plants at the beginning and end of the season: rude tough spears or weedy sprue. The stock is made from nourishing nettle tops, tiny new potatoes and leeks, virtually the only other vegetables growing in the garden at the moment.

Finely chop and fry a few leeks in butter with a couple of potatoes in a deep pan. Add the asparagus and a bag of nettle tops, collected and tentatively trimmed from their stalks, wearing gloves. It's worth mentioning, to the uninitiated, stinging nettles lose their sting when boiled. Sweat and dilute with stock, boiling till the potatoes are soft. Season and liquidize, reheating with a tablespoon of lemon juice and crème fraîche.

After a while, cooked asparagus goes a dreary khaki colour. If you can't serve this soup straight away, save a few tender young green stems to whiz up and add just before serving. A surprisingly delicate, nourishing late spring tonic, full of protein and vitamins.

In full season, I eat asparagus greedily, whenever I can – steamed, grilled, and quite often raw, (as I walk past the bed, if there's a single spear), but my all time favourite lunch consists of just a few choice shoots, steamed with their tough base stem left on, for easy dipping into soft boiled eggs, with a slice of home baked bread and a few shavings of pecorino cheese, eaten in the sun in the garden with the hens as my companions, hoping for the crumbs.

Many of the best meals I've ever eaten have come from food, rather than recipes. You walk into a shop, see an ingredient that's at its best, you imagine it would taste good, add a herb or a spice, you take it home and cook it. Your vegetable garden can become your supermarket, with your trug as a trolley. You can wander through, see a plant that is approaching its peak, (though not necessarily the peak of its growth, younger is often better) pop it in your basket, think that would taste good with dill, or coriander, pick some from the herb garden, go into the kitchen and cook it, as simply as possible. And eat it.

Restaurant chefs' recipes are often complicated, and fail if even one of the ingredients escapes us. Often though, another seasonal item will do the trick. Sometimes, being told exactly what to do by someone else – an expert, takes away our own innate cooking abilities, and the chance to make a dish our own. I'm more a Ray Mears fan than Gordon Ramsay, anyway.

My culinary hero, Jane Grigson, liked to cook new potatoes with her asparagus. I would add mint. They are all at their best now. This is a perfect marriage: the asparagus benefit from the support of the potatoes in the pot, they are improved by the flavour of the asparagus and both are enhanced by the mint. A symbiotic relationship not unlike the one between hens and the veggie garden: the hens eat the trimmings and leftovers (and without judicious caging, the whole bang shoot) and the beds are liberally manured

123

and cleaned up in the autumn. But we are especially lucky to get an extra bonus – the eggs.

This is my 'recipe' for couscous, peas and broad beans with soft boiled eggs, mint and chervil. I'm aware, as I stagger in from a day's gardening with people to feed, that both energy and sugar levels are at a low ebb, especially after a glass of wine, so this quick and easy filling supper can also be made – under instruction – by other members of the family, able to take a hint.

Pour a jug of boiling water mixed with a teaspoon of Marigold stock over a plate of couscous, following the maker's proportions and instructions. Steam a few fresh peas and beans with mint in a steamer over the boiling eggs and add to the couscous. Add the peeled halved eggs and a sprinkling of chervil. (The latter was not a popular addition, and was picked off some plates, but I liked it).

23rd

Discover a nest of small white eggs hidden in our narrow strip of front garden. They belong to one of the pair of next door's Old English Game bantams. These bright beady-eyed birds, with their typical flat-iron silhouette, have decided that despite the Cockerel's lack of enthusiasm, the grass is greener on this side of the fence. It has taken two years for them to be tolerated by the Orpingtons. With great subtlety, they have integrated themselves – though tactfully they sleep in the ivy covered bushes by the backdoor and make themselves scarce at mealtimes, nipping in only to finish any leftovers. In nature, the flock would not only be protecting its territory and food sources from outsiders, but its members' health from imported disease, to which they could be vulnerable. We hen keepers expect a lot from our flocks when we introduce newcomers, hoping they'll be accepted just to please us. Just one of the reasons I prefer to hatch my own additions to the flock.

PS. When the eggs were floated later in a bowl of water, they all rose promptly to the surface, proving they were probably rather ancient, so they were binned.

28th

Off to bed with a hot water bottle. How can it be so cold? How do the animals and birds cope with these ridiculous plummeting temperatures? However nippy it is at night, I have to sleep with the window open. Even in the house, I need a connection with outside. This place was originally designed twenty five years ago with no internal doors, apart from the loos, but teenage demands for privacy have meant a few adjustments. Even so, my part of the house is still open plan with views of the garden, and the landscape beyond with plenty of escape routes.

29th

The ancient lime trees surrounding the churchyard are in full leaf. There are twelve, said to represent the apostles. I treasure an early photograph from 1906 showing these trees in their untrammelled majesty. Nowadays they are regularly butchered and pollarded by the church and other interested parties. This over-zealous pruning encourages basal growth, leaving boles like huge warts with sprouting hairs, and we end up with a truncated hedge of vigorous shoots, and in winter, a line of distorted massacred torsos.

One of my first memories of this house was at Easter. We looked out through a curtain of barely leafing lime twigs to a flock of sheep grazing in the churchyard. They seemed to me to be symbolically perfect biblical lawn mowers, cheap and efficient, but the parishioners complained of nibbled snacks among the floral dedications and of sheep poo on the pathway. So the strimmer reigns. And on the subject of snacks, I'm told that very young lime leaves taste good in a spring salad.

30th

A good day's weeding in the vegetable garden. All the veggie seedlings are out of their pots and snugly planted in beds, protected from the hens with low wooden netted cages (that double up as coops for the chicks), or with bamboo cloches, or plastic bell jars, netted tunnels, anything to discourage further rummaging in the soil. Speaking of the hens, they celebrate this lovely afternoon with a massive communal dustbath in the spot where we light our annual bonfires.

The contented clucks and the frantic scratching and heaving, attracts next door's bantams, who are at first excluded on the grounds that, even after all this time, they are complete strangers. Finally though, one by one, in an aura of *bonhomie*, they are let in, until they all writhe in an ecstasy of feathered delight and a cloud of wood ash. The cat and I watch intently, and having worked and weeded our way through the vigorously sprouting artichokes and cardoons, through the leeks with their goblin-like buds growing haphazardly throughout the plot, we collect the last few broad beans, and head exhausted for the house.

Have just enough energy to boil a small pan of pasta, steam a handful of broad beans in a steamer on top (with their jackets off, because these are rather elderly) and serve together with a dollop of crème fraîche and chopped mint and chives.

31st

Defra has not found any links between the three Norfolk poultry units infected by H5N7, except their closeness to one another. Domestic poultry and feed sources have been eliminated and they are now focusing on wild birds, visitors, and foxes dragging carcasses from one farm to another, which seems pretty unlikely.

It's a great relief that the infection hasn't spread across the area, and my heart goes out to those families whose livelihoods were affected and whose flocks were slaughtered. Sadly, we've been affected in a minor way by the tragedy too. Book sales are down this year by two thirds, people are naturally put off keeping hens and course attendance has suffered. A magazine has cancelled one of the hen keeping courses they were planning to hold here. They even asked my insurers if my policy covered students catching avian flu. I hear of henhouse manufacturers laying off staff and breeders going out of business, we are all lesser casualties of this insidious disease and, to be truthful, of the media frenzy surrounding the whole sorry business.

JUNE

Tarragon & Dill

Cow Parsley

Old Fashioned Roses

Bees Buzzing

Elderflower Cordial

Hen Keeping Courses

Limeflower Tisane

1st

Troston is an unremarkable village of about 400 inhabitants, a ten minute drive from Bury St Edmunds. Sitting not so prettily between the Ixworth prairies and sandy Brecklands, the area is bounded by the huge Euston estate and a military no-mans' land. We have no shop, no school, a charmless pub with regularly changing landlords, and a huge wool church which overshadows our plot and overwhelms the regular congregation of eight.

Built of odds and ends, Church Cottage was originally the cart house for the church opposite, where wealthy parishioners left their transport under shelter while they worshipped. Converted parsimoniously into a pair of labourers' cottages, two up, two down and then into a bungalow, we bought it as weekenders a quarter of a century ago. Now much extended and our permanent family home for the last 20 years or so, it is sheltered from the north winds by its massive Gothic neighbour, overlooks open fields to the south and east and is bordered by the farmer's tied cottages – now rented, to the west. Down a leafy cul-de-sac that peters off to a footpath, the lane and cottage have a peaceful atmosphere and after a lifetime of regularly changing addresses, we've finally come home.

2nd

Double cream has colour-washed the June countryside. The lanes are fringed with a frill of cow parsley, which has invaded my garden through the euphemistic whimsy we call the Meadow – the Verge would suit it better. Initially a dream of ox-eye daisies, poppies, cornflowers and selected grasses, this part of the garden soon deteriorated into a tangle of *umbelliferae*, teasels, dead nettles and a rather pretty blue cranesbill. Fleetingly very romantic, like the roadsides, it soon disintegrates into rank

133

wilderness. The birds enjoy the seeds, so the final cut is deferred and it gets worse every year. I have dreams of growing birches, under-planted with bluebells.

Although finally looking established, after 25 years, I still plan a few changes to the garden. Happy with my original design, I'd love to simplify the planting, preferring a visually more cohesive outline, with fewer flowers, and perhaps even the introduction, horror of horrors, of more shrubs.

Low maintenance is a sad concept, and edible plants hardly fall into that category (some end up using more energy to plant and harvest, than calories gained when eaten) but as years go by, I'm losing interest in plants that offer nothing other than a visual feast. We all have to earn our keep.

3rd

The little black hen, known as the Nasty Hen, has hatched out one Orpington chick. Queen of mums, she chaperones her baby to the best spots to dustbathe, to ants' nests where swarms of protein send the hens into a frenzy, and to the compost heaps to scratch about and sunbathe. She's not really nasty, just unimpressed by people. Unlike the Orpingtons who, when approached, come fluttering towards me like fat moths, she shoots off fast in the opposite direction. After eight years of care, it's a bit dispiriting. Let's hope the chick doesn't inherit her foster mum's temperament.

134

Watching the flock, you can see why, traditionally, cocks have been symbols of power and virility (though the title of avian Lothario should go to the notoriously badly behaved Mallard drake - the only bird with a penis). The hen, meanwhile is a model of pre-feminist womanhood: productive, housewifely and modest. Our cockerel keeps a wary eye open, clucking to call his ladies if he finds food and then stands back while they eat, like a host at a banquet, until dusk when he leads them home to roost.

Hens can't see in the dark, so they always head for home as light fades. Ducks and other waterfowl sleep with one eye open and half of their brain alert to danger – a good trick, but one that consequently makes them impossible to chaperone to safety as night falls. I'm told the way to lure them in, is to only ever feed them in the evening in their bedchambers and then quickly shut the door.

9th

I suppose this is the main garden's zenith, the culmination of a year's labour, with still a few good things to come. To be truthful, I prefer early spring: that fresh lime green is the colour that excites me. That's why we grow so many euphorbias, coupled with royal blue grape hyacinths, zingy magenta honesty and vibrant orange marigolds; these are colours that intoxicate. But June's pale pinks and lavenders will do. With several articles about the Kitchen Garden appearing in magazines, visitor numbers rocket. What nice people garden (and chicken) lovers are. Always polite, inquisitive – though why does curiosity always breed the same questions? Guests come, wander round the garden, gasp with astonishment at the Orpington's size, enjoy their tea and cake, buy a card or two, a book perhaps and a pot of jam and then wend their way, wondering who on earth that dotty woman thinks she is. I don't charge an entrance fee, I'm not confident enough of my garden's charms.

Things may have to change though, with wider publicity and more visitors, I've noticed a propensity to just have the tea and cake and dispense with the purchases. Realistically, I have to make a living.

The garden is smallish – two thirds of an acre – usually casually scruffy. I garden with the blessed help of Nigel who cuts the grass once a week, but mostly it's me, with lots of competition for my time. It's no great shakes – none of the amazing cascades, follies and mazes that most gardens that open to the public feel they have to supply to a quickly bored public, used to seeing instant makeovers. We have no ridiculously unrealistic Chelsea plant combinations and the whole isn't the result of hundreds of years of growth with tens of gardeners' labour.

This is a glimpse of a small domestic landscape. A visit is just a snapshot of twenty odd years of design, cultivation, plus a little money, but mostly the result of our own creativity and hard work. For some, only a minority sadly, it is exactly their cup of tea. I can spot them, sense their delight and have made some really good friends.

Often people come to check whether it really is possible to keep hens in a garden, and still keep the garden looking reasonable. To be truthful, of course it would be easier without those pecking beaks, scratching claws and smelly deposits, but I would be losing drama, colour, interest, and compost. Now when I visit homes without some kind of avian livestock, it seems two dimensional, flat, and to be truthful, soulless and boring.

But to be realistic, it takes management and planning. Ratios of birds to space need to be calculated. Start with a few, and never allow your passion to let you overstock. Choice of breed is extremely important. My short list of successful garden hens now includes: Brahmas, Cochins and Orpingtons (in all their various colourways) and for those who prefer smaller birds – Pekins, Silkies and Wyandottes. The better the layer, the less help they are in the garden. Forgo free range hens, if you are a plantsman, bedding plant fanatic, serious self-sufficiency fan, or are squeamish or house proud. Let *laisser-faire* be your watchword and concentrate on the positive aspects: the occasional egg, beautiful plumage, companionship and goings-on worthy of a soap opera.

Garden hen keepers come to the hobby as a progression from vegetable gardening, from a desire to provide and nurture both their birds and their families. Hardly surprising then, that we've all been so shocked by the worry that maybe we are putting our family's health at risk by keeping hens. In the commercial world – where I believe avian influenza has originated – it is abuse that has caused this disease. I believe that our birds, kept in near perfect natural conditions, should escape this plague. There is evidence however, that they might still become infected by wild birds and not show symptoms, but be infectious. All still to be proved.

12th

Decide Henkeepers' Association website should go on-line free to subscribers. That whatever information we put out should be accessible to all, in order to get a true reflection of the pro-vaccination support and help as many people as possible.

14th

Hen keeping course.

COUNTING YOUR CHICKENS.

Eleven students, mostly ladies, though sometimes with a reluctant husband or two in tow, come to learn:
All there is to know about keeping hens:
with hands-on advice, practical tips,
and a fabulous slide show.
Meet our famous flock of Orpingtons
and see them in action,
plus on-site hints on how to garden despite your hens.
Includes a visit from breeder Hugh Burton
and his award winning Silkie hen - Showgirl.
All topped off with a home-grown lunch, a glass of wine,
and an afternoon chat with cook Penelope Hands,
who will show you how to cook delicious recipes using
your own hens' eggs.

And that's exactly what we do. It's usually a very pleasant day spent with jolly people enjoying themselves, delighted to be among others equally obsessed with chickens.

We have done this course at Elizabeth Barrett Browning's elegant house at Hope End in Herefordshire (she wasn't

there); at a decommissioned country railway station in the hills of Northumberland, supported by a magician of a bantam breeder, who produced, from a series of cardboard boxes, a dozen very similar black and white birds I'd never seen before in my life; and at a restored water mill in Constable country, while the owner's flock of wild chickens glared at us from the surrounding trees. I really enjoy myself because I'm allowed talk on a subject I really love, with no real danger of boring my audience.

16th

Beauty's chicks are about six weeks old and she has decided they are old enough to fend for themselves. She smoothes down her blowsy broody feathers, like an instant post-natal diet, and the chicks no longer recognize her slimmer silhouette. Nature severs the tie – instant adolescence. She stops sleeping with them in the broody hut and goes back to the henhouse with the others.

Strangely enough, the Old Hen and her daughter have always been inseparable. Three years on, they still hang out together. The chick even waited outside the nest in the old days, as her mum laid her daily egg. They preen each other, chat *à deux* and sunbathe together in the sunniest spots. When the daughter went broody last year, mum was inconsolable and hung around outside the nest, patiently passing time till she emerged.

Though still protected by the Cockerel and tolerated by the rest of the flock, this year's adolescents lead an independent life, with just a little supervision from me. This way, they grow up as part of the troupe and won't suffer the trauma and downright nastiness reserved for outsiders and newcomers. They're still at the bottom of the pecking order, but with time, and probably a lot of favouritism from the Cockerel as they come on-lay, they'll have a bearable time with not too many others above them in the pecking order, picking on them.

18th

The old-fashioned roses flower and fade. Make the most of their fleeting beauty and bring bunches into the house. I love apricot 'Gloire de Dijon' that grows under the bedroom window, dark, dark red velvet climbing 'Guinée', and those delicious French ladies: Mesdames 'Alfred Carrière', 'Albertine' and 'Zéphirine Drouhin', but my favourite is 'Cuisse de Nymphe Emue', prudishly translated by the Victorians as 'Great Maiden's Blush'. If ever there was a barometer of trans-channel sensuality, this is it. Are the petals the colour of a maiden's blush, or the seductive tint of her thigh, or better still – the blush of her skin in ecstasy? In a tumbler, on the bedside table, the perfume lasts even as the petals fall.

19th

Not all June's bounty smells so sweetly. How can blossom with a bouquet of cat pee make such delicately flavoured nectar? We have always offered our customers elderflower cordial, and my friend Rena has finally come up with the definitive recipe: light, lemony and Muscat flavoured:

Pick 10 flowery heads on a sunny day and soak them in 1½pints/850ml of boiled cooled water in a large pan or bucket. Add 1½ lbs/750g of sugar (I like light muscovado – but the colour is less attractive) and 3-4 sliced lemons with their juice and zest. Leave to macerate for 24-48 hours and then strain through a muslin-lined sieve.

This recipe keeps well in the fridge, but can be saved and frozen in small plastic bottles. I went to a children's birthday party a while ago and noticed some pretty, homemade jellies made of elderflower cordial with blueberries floating in them. We use it to flavour gooseberry fools, water ices, and our now famous Elderflower, Lemon and Sweet Cicely Sponge.

Take a good Madeira or sponge cake still warm from the oven and drizzle the surface liberally with cordial, so like a sponge, it soaks up the liquid. Cover with grated lemon zest, dredge with icing sugar and decorate with sweet cicely leaves. For a really special occasion (gilding the lily slightly), layer the sponge with a greedy filling of lemon curd mixed with mascarpone. This cake has turned customers into friends.

Once used to flavour Chartreuse, sweet cicely is too prolific for the herb garden, so has been banished to grow wild in the meadow, where it seeds itself happily. The delicate ferns can be added to tart fruits – gooseberries and rhubarb – as a pleasant way to reduce their acid bite. Angelica has the same effect, and seeds itself with the same abandon, but its statuesque beauty reserves it a place in the flower garden.

The summer herbs, potted tarragon, and coriander and dill, grown in the vegetable garden in rows, are at their best now. If you are fond of the taste of tarragon, try this recipe.

Wrap a newly laid egg in tarragon leaves, cover with cling film and leave in the fridge for 24 hours. Boil for a soft-boiled egg with a delicious difference. Tarragon is the perfect partner for eggs. I like to cook runny scrambled eggs, flavoured with tarragon and topped with gooey grated Gruyère cheese.

With the promise of hundreds of recipes inside their cleverly designed packaging, like all things of value, eggs should be treated with care. Eggshells are porous, so avoid storing them near other pungent ingredients, like lemons and garlic. If you are organizing your harvest correctly and eating your eggs fresh, don't worry about keeping them in the fridge. Store them pointy end down in a cool larder or on the work surface. If you doubt an egg's freshness, pop it in a bowl of water, if fresh, it will sink. As an egg ages the air sac enlarges, so an old one will float. Always date your eggs with a soft pencil, I find even fibre pens can affect that special eggy flavour.

Keep your freshest eggs to poach, scramble and boil (though a 5 day old hard boiled egg is easier to peel). Save the older ones for baking. Despite having had a bad few years, the health lobby now consider eggs to be a perfect food with the right kind of dietary cholesterol, packed full of protein (6 grams), vitamins D and B2, iodine and beneficial fats. According to the Food Standards Agency, most of us can eat them with impunity.

So, use them with imagination, they are the most versatile ingredient in your larder. Soufflés, mousses and meringues; sauces: mayonnaise, béarnaise and hollandaise; pasta, frittatas and omelettes; ice creams, custards and sorbets; marzipan, curds and nougat - many of the world's most delicious dishes rely on the mysterious alchemy within the egg's shell.

146

20th

Big increase in Henkeepers' Association membership. Up to 10 new subscribers a day. I carry on writing to Defra, as do all the other poultry keeping pressure groups: the caged birds aficionados – worried for their canaries, budgies and parrots; the Turkey Club members, headed by the redoubtable Janice Houghton-Wallace; the various water and wildfowl associations with so much to lose; the Poultry Club, whose shows in the past have been cancelled; and all the individual breed clubs.

Most vociferous of them all is writer Dr. Christine Ashton of the Call Duck Association, to whom all the above owe a huge debt of gratitude for keeping us all so well informed by email.

I update the website regularly, not just with the gloom and doom of avian flu updates, and replies from letters to Ministers and Shadow Ministers, but with snippets of info on egg producers and suppliers. Did you know Waitrose was selling bantam eggs in boxes of four for £1.60? There are red mite alerts, with a list of tried and tested remedies in the Products section and feeding tips, with the news that Sainsbury's is selling cheap frozen sweet corn in packs; ideal for hens.

I write a monthly blog on what's happening In the Run, hot for this month – info on chick feed: "grind up sunflower seeds in an old coffee grinder" and a reminder to members to relax in the garden with their flocks. And In the Garden: remember to cloche your strawberries. In the Kitchen: I suggest our recipe for tarragon boiled egg. I believe eventually all magazines will appear on-line.

21st

If I just had a tiny garden, I would grow herbs in pots, keep a couple of pretty bantams for eggs and company and grow salads in a small raised bed. People often say they have no space to grow vegetables, but many are beautiful enough to plant in amongst the flowers and shrubs, though mine would have to be cloched so that the bantams didn't dine on them before I did.

My favourite vegetable flowers are leeks, and I grow them dotted about in groups of half a dozen in the middle ground of the border. Their striking blue/purple/green foliage, absurd pointy buds and pinkish multi-flowered heads are good enough value for pride of place. Their only drawback is a malodorous oniony smell.

Other veg that successfully make a decorative leap from potager to flowerbed are the kales - 'Redbor' and 'Cavolo Nero', artichokes and cardoons, purple or yellow podded French dwarf beans, beetroot 'Bull's Blood' and sprouting broccoli, and all the multi-colour stemmed chards. Chicories look stunning throughout the winter, especially 'Rosso di Treviso', and hearted lettuces like 'Quatre Saisons' are pretty as posies in the front of the border.

Many of the chillis, like 'Fiesta' or 'Hungarian Hot Wax' look stunning in pots in rows along a sunny outside window ledge or in a window box. I draw the line at hanging baskets, but edible foliage and flowers have got to be an improvement on the ubiquitous petunia.

Pumpkins, squashes and gourds can curl along fences and scramble over hedges, while runner bean 'Painted Lady' merits a place on a trellis, and herbs dill and fennel, angelica and garlic chives, chervil and borage will self-seed themselves happily and not look out of place in a cottage garden.

On the other hand, there are many annual flowers that look stunning in rows ranged alongside your vegetables, hopefully distracting pests like carrot fly and caterpillars at the same time. Pot marigolds, nasturtiums - especially Black Velvet, (both of which taste good in salads) feverfew, and Love-in-a-Mist interlope happily and not too greedily in the veg plot.

22nd

The lime trees are covered in fragrant blossom and the bees are working hard. Limeflower honey is said to be the most sought-after, certainly the flavour is one of the most delicate.

This honey ice cream would be fragrantly delicious if the sweetness came from sticky lime or acacia flower honey.

Bring a pint/600ml of single cream to boiling point. Carefully add 4 beaten egg yolks to the mixture while stirring, then strain it through a sieve back into the saucepan. Warm the mixture over a low heat, whisking till thick enough to coat the back of a spoon. Stir in 6oz/180g of warmed liquid honey.

Leave the custard to cool and mix in ¼ pt/125ml of Greek yoghurt. Scoop into your ice cream maker and follow instructions.

Common or garden honey ice cream can be enlivened with lavender flowers, left to steep in the warmed cream and then strained out before freezing. Or just pour a couple of gooey tablespoons of honey over best vanilla ice cream for a quick pud, and add chopped stem ginger for a special treat.

This recipe for Valerie's Plain Honey Cake comes from Penny's book, *Beekeeping for Beginners*.

Melt 4oz/125g of soft brown sugar, 5oz/150g unsalted butter, 6oz/180g honey with a tablespoon of water over a moderate heat till dissolved. Whisk in 2 beaten eggs and 7oz/210g self-raising flour till smooth.

Pour into an 8 inch greased and lined tin and bake in a moderate oven for an hour. Cool and top with lemon icing.

Several years ago, I acquired a hive of bees and took on a mentor to see me through the first season. Sadly, he was not often available to help (it turned out he was a pilot), and left unmanaged, satellites from my hive swarmed next door to their 30ft high Christmas tree with regular monotony, disturbing barbecues, so they had to go.

I have strong summer memories of the drone of bees, the scent of the limeflowers and the slightly drippy green shade that the branches shed on the interior of this cottage. These can instantly be evoked later on in the year by drinking a cup of golden limeflower tisane. The flowers should be picked and dried now and stored in airtight jars to conjure up memories of the month of June, as the year declines.

23rd

Five years ago, almost to the day, I was chatting to some customers when we were interrupted by a phone call from a sailing buddy of my husband's. He said Jean-François had suffered some kind of fit. They would call back. A lifetime later they rang again. I was told to come to Ipswich hospital.

Through the interminable journey along the A14 and round endless roundabouts ringing the outskirts of town, I tried to tell myself this wasn't happening, I made deals with God. It wasn't until we arrived in the foyer, I learned that Jean had suffered a massive heart attack on the boat and despite the valiant efforts of his friends, the rescue helicopter crew and the casualty staff, he had died.

The hospital procedures and funeral arrangements, the police, solicitors, registrars are all a blur, but somehow or another we must have navigated our way through the following six months, looking to all the world like normal people.

No-one should die in summer. Every year at this time, even now, a painful gloom settles in for the month – a gloom that creeps up like a fugue, and then the red poppies on the verges remind me why I'm gloomy, but this doesn't make it better. I still struggle daily, and five years on, the pain replaced by a dull ache, it seems unbelievable that a healthy, life-loving, enthusiast set off for a weekend's sailing and didn't come back. I miss him most for our sons. He should be here, enjoying their successes and helping with their problems. But he *is* here, in them. From Jean *le débrouillard*, they have inherited resourcefulness, legendary skill and good humour.

155

Somehow, the wind was taken out of his sails. That lucky zephyr that propelled him breezily through life just blew itself out.

JULY

High Summer

Salad Leaves

Sweet Berries

Ice Creams & Sorbets

Clucking Hens

Morello Cherry Jam

Swimming Pools

1st

The rising barometer brings back hazy memories of Jean's wake. On a perfect summer's day, at a venue chosen more for its stunning location on the banks of the estuary, than any culinary reputation, I remember looking down at a paper plate covered with custard creams and hula hoops – standard fare for a funeral tea apparently. Jean's opinion of English food finally validated.

Hoarse from shouting above the wail of a jazz band to long lost friends, we listened to the humanist preacher's eulogy – our vicar from the church opposite could have said the same things – but Jean, vehemently irreligious, would have turned in his watery grave. The ultimate betrayal though: we couldn't save the other half of his ashes, returned to his family in Montreal, from a high pomp Catholic burial, but funerals are for the living after all, not the dead.

Three of his mates – fair-weather friends, who haven't been seen since – gave heart-breaking valedictory speeches, while helicopters droned noisily overhead. Jean had been airlifted to hospital from his boat, so every time we are plagued with air manoeuvres from the local airfield – we remember him. Not that we ever need reminding – this place remains a testament to his style, endeavour and goodwill.

Through the shocks and changes of life, the garden provides constancy. Although weather patterns are less predictable nowadays, the inevitability of the seasons forms the backbone – and backdrop – to all my endeavours. The routine of the birds' daily rhythm is my own timetable. The early morning cacophony of cock, hens and ducks, punctuated with the staccato calls of the moorhen, is my alarm.

With the hens fed at the crack of dawn, I usually go back to bed to daydream. I eat my healthy breakfast of ground flax seeds, walnuts, oatflakes and grated pear with cinnamon - pretty similar to the stuff I've just served up to the hens. Then with superhuman effort, I go and have a swim or get dressed to stagger up the lane. There are signs of human life: dog walkers, early risers, the postman, with luck – though he's usually much later – and once a week the apocalyptic coming of the binmen with flashing lights and a rush of noise and clatter. The daily routine rolls on, we all get swept along.

2nd

Midsummer has passed, and so have the garden's glory days. Although still a riot of colour – too much for my palette, we're on the downward run. The big show gardens replace their perennials like bedding plants, two or three times a season, but in doing so, they lose July's blowsy charm, accelerated this year by a heatwave.

The grass is dessicated brown, and 'Kiftsgate', the last rose to flower overwhelms its apple tree host. The milkweed thistles have already shed their seed, greedily gobbled up by the chickens. How do they know it has beneficial properties for the liver? The jasmine's breath-taking fragrance, best inhaled from a distance, perfumes the house at dusk and my beautiful potted lilies have been attacked by lily beetle. Disgusting grubs encased in their own excrement, how can anything that preys on such elegance be so gross?

160

The flowers may be expiring in a wave of intoxicating perfume, but the veg plot is reaching its productive zenith. We carry the kitchen table out on to the terrace, next to the terracotta outdoor oven, but thank heavens, the best summer meals don't need to be cooked.

At lunchtime I set off to the salad bed, where, quick to bolt in this heat and protected from my flock in low netted cages, grow rows of pretty salad leaves. From dark red beetroot tops, through pink chenopodium, to all shades of green: fern-like dill to crisp pak choi; from lemony buckler-leaved sorrel to the bitter chicories, narrow toothed bucks horn 'Erba Stella' and floppy buttery lettuce leaves, all augmented with handfuls of wild rocket, basil, coriander, mint and parsley from the herb garden; young chard leaves, asparagus tips and blanched French beans from the vegetable plot, enriched with pumpkin seeds, pine nuts and hardboiled eggs from the larder – and, in times of paucity, with packs of saladini from the supermarket.

Having spent an exhaustingly hot afternoon filling a trugful of berries and the last of the peas, I smugly podded, topped and tailed and sorted while watching the World Cup final. I felt my efforts at least equalled those of Zidane and company, but judging by my son's acid comments – bucking the general trend of young allotment growers – this could be the last generation of Raymonds to grow much of this produce.

He enjoyed his supper though. A risotto with peas, lemon and ricotta and herbs.

Combine 8oz/225g ricotta with plenty of chopped parsley, garlic chives and basil. Add as much lemon zest as you like and season with salt and pepper (we occasionally eat this mixture as a dip with batons of cucumber, celery or carrot). Cook 10oz/300g of good risotto rice, adding a cupful of fresh peas at the last moment. Drain, but leave the rice quite wet and spoon in the ricotta mixture. Top with grated parmesan.

3rd

A conversation via 'Skype' with Jacques and Saskia working on a film recreating an Alaskan village in New Zealand. With pop star-type headphone/speaker apparatus and camera, we can see and hear them, free of charge, sitting in their apartment in Auckland, drinking a bottle of chilled New Zealand white, while bleary eyed, twelve hours ahead we sip our early morning tea. Afterwards, I feel strangely cheated, a virtual meeting, however welcome, is not the real thing and I miss them more than ever.

4th

I don't usually give my hens names. Not because I don't love them, or recognize them as individuals, but simply because having named them, I can never quite remember who's who when I need to. Nowadays this amnesia extends to children, cats, friends, (and my own name, if I'm honest). So my flock has generic nomenclature. The girls are all called 'Babe' or 'Girlie' or 'Beauty' or whatever passes as an endearment at the moment and we are on to Cockerel Mk V.

However, the Araucana chicks we hatched out for a friend last year (a new brooding service we offer, along with adopt-a-flock, home-a-rooster and rent-a-cockerel) were so different to their large round blond cousins, they were christened immediately. The lavender pullet just had to be Violet, and her brother with exotic markings, dark glasses and a Latin look, was obviously Alfonso, both hot to dance the Argentinian tango.

Later, it turned out that Alfonso, was in fact Alphonsine. Which was just as well. Extra cockerels aren't welcome in the chicken coop. Poor things. I plan, when I'm old and disgraceful, to keep just cockerels. They get on pretty well together without hens and they are so beautiful. And much more interesting than the females, who are far too busy. There's just the crowing. Troston be warned!

Many of the families who come to visit, enthusiastically reel off their flocks' roll call of names, and it's great to see how much fun children get from these pets. I often recommend Pekins and Silkies, breeds available in several different colours, so that each child can instantly recognize their favourite. Anyone who has kept hens knows that far from being the brain-dead clones the battery farming industry would have us believe, they have very particular characters and it's easy to tell them apart.

There is new research out from an Australian university, proving that chickens communicate through a wide range of language, can recognize individual members of their flock and have good retentive memory – all of which any hen keeper could have told them. The professor added that when he gives his paper, he reads this list of attributes before mentioning which species he's talking about. The audience always assume he's about to lecture on the subject of apes.

Apart from their most obvious call – the crow, cocks also sing, a soft, not particularly melodic song, when all is well. They have a striking alarm call that other members of the flock take up, building up to a pretty deafening crescendo, and during the mating season, on finding food, the male will muster his hens to him, in a *basso* version of the *staccato* 'tuk tuk' a mum uses to encourage her babes to eat.

Most of my laying ladies will cackle triumphantly when they have laid an egg, cluck contentedly generally, squawk when angry, and those are just the bits of their language we understand. It suits us to believe that all the species we eat are insentient creatures, and many people never make the connection between pork and pigs, beef and cows, and packets of chicken breasts with hens.

11th

Plagued with thrips and thunderbugs on a hot airless afternoon, I lie in the garden on the ancient swing seat, surrounded by hens, various ducks and my patient cat. Looking up into the dappled shady realms of the walnut tree, this is my proudest horticultural achievement, planted 21 years ago. This sprouted nut, barely taller than the surrounding meadow grass, started life in a spot where the orphaned ducklings paddled and dabbled, manured and watered, giving this magnificent tree a fertile start in life. Flanked by an avenue of yew, now 3ft thick and 10 ft tall leading on to the vista of a borrowed landscape beyond – delusions of grandeur through a rickety iron gate – it's my

favourite part of the garden, I'd happily forgo the rest for this peaceful shady spot.

I've put out a huge French galvanized pan, originally used, I think as a dairy skimmer, now full of water for this year's hatch of ducklings to preen, duck and dive. If only they didn't make such a mess. It's so easy to get immersed in their lives. I'm mesmerized by their burbling and preening – they work their way through every tiny feather. Totally interbred, a glorious hotch potch of Call Duck, Aylesburys and Campbells, Runners, Magpie and the ever promiscuous Mallard. Each duck has different markings, giving identity to their characters, so it's easy to make favourites and spot villains. Some make wonderful mothers with patient beaux, others go hopelessly scattering babes all over the village.

During the summer hols, when the boys were young, we would take on orphan birds. We all had persistently cheeping little fledglings in our pockets, and soon got a reputation in the village – I was the Duck Lady, long before I became the Chicken Woman. People would bring birds from far and wide.

The most difficult was Ludwig, (we had already been through most of the other composers). He was a tiny partridge who peeped incessantly for three days and nights, in my ear – he thought the nape of my neck was the cosiest place to live. In the end, I could stand it no longer, and he was slipped into a brood of partridge chicks in an incubator, but I never held out much hope, I'm afraid.

It is possible to raise abandoned ducklings, especially in small groups. They keep each other warm with the help of an anglepoise lamp, and are company for one another. We had great success in returning them to the main flock in the autumn, when they were fully grown. Mallard grow as you watch, but throughout the summer holidays, we were 'Mum'. If the phone rang while you were gardening, and you rushed in, so did they. Eventually, I found a lad who took them on each year, until he reached adolescence and found other interests. Now I have to harden my heart. We are already overwhelmed.

The resident pair of moorhens and their chicks come out to graze, the parents wisely pinking warnings of the cats's presence. She's queen of cats for abstaining from chicks and ducklings - she knows they're family, but can't resist these little black leggy blobs. The female gallantly rebuilds her nest on the pontoon and lays another clutch.

I listen to blackbirds, the buzz of bees on the lime flowers, the sonar quacks of mother ducks and babes communicating, the constant flap and coo of woodpigeons and canoodling collared doves, all making the background music to my life. We really don't hear much else, especially since Max has found a full time job in a studio in Bury: a distant dog, the breeze through next door's Christmas tree, the drone of the inevitable strimmer and the occasional cargo plane full of burgers *en route* to Mildenhall airbase.

16th

High summer in a heatwave: tall corn, dried, parched plants, dessicated roses, discarded ducks' down, and the overpowering scent of buddleia. Doggedly, I water my pot plants with washing up water and siphon the bathwater through a hose into the veg beds. This area has been spared the hosepipe ban, but we're metered and try to preserve water. Then over the road decides to hose down all his white, plastic garden furniture......

It's too hot. Mums and chicks are lying in the shade of the fruit bushes, keeping a hopeful eye open for the odd falling berry. Miraculously the hens have never discovered just how good the wild Alpine strawberries *Fragaria* Semperflorens *vesca* are. These neat plants edge the beds in the pompously named cutting garden and don't runner promiscuously like most wild strawberries. Just a few tiny berries scattered in a dish of fat bloated cultivated berries, lifts the flavour back to childhood, when strawberries were strawberries.

All the berries and currants ripen in a glut and need to be picked quickly and turned into sorbets, ice creams or sauces. My favourites are the dessert gooseberries from a venerable, lichen covered plant, given to me by Mr. Clark, one of the oldest inhabitants of the village, which I race the hens to eat straight from the bush. The rest are best fooled and poached in elderflower cordial until soft. Strained and cooled, and spooned into thick cream, Greek yoghurt or, best of all, a luxurious home made custard.

Making custard is almost a lost art, but one worth reviving.

Separate two eggs and beat the yolks with two tablespoons of vanilla sugar. Heat ¼ pint/150ml of milk and gently pour into the egg and sugar mixture. Cook over the lowest heat, slowly stirring until creamy and thick. Cool and add to any berry pureé for a sumptuous pud, or freeze in a gelatiére to make ice cream.

We train all our currants to grow as standards. Ruthless pruning back to just one leader right from the start, encourages bushy growth at the top of the plant, leaving space underneath for other veg, and keeps the berries out of reach of certain flightless feathery fruit lovers.

Pride of place goes to the jostaberries, a vigorous cross between the goosegog and blackcurrant. These make an excellent cordial with one pint of strained juice sweetened with 1lb of sugar. Any surplus can be cooled, poured into small plastic bottles and frozen. This elixir can also be used to flavour water ices by adding the beaten egg whites left over from your custard or mixed with indifferent white wine to make Kir. All the currants make delicious juices and sorbets as well as jams and jellies.

This sorbet uses blackcurrant leaves as an unusual flavouring for a water ice.

Melt 4oz/125g caster sugar in ½ pint/200ml of boiling water. Steep and simmer a large handful of blackcurrant leaves in the syrup and leave to cool. Add the juice and zest of a couple of lemons and freeze. Beat in a beaten egg white and freeze again. Decorate with a few currants.

Penny makes a similar ice cream using scented geranium (pelargonium) leaves, suggesting we use lemon or rose scented varieties, and avoid the apple scented Pelargonium *Odoratissimum*, that smells like cheap soap.

Wash and dry 8 leaves and put them in a stainless steel saucepan with 12floz/375ml whipping cream and

172

4floz/125ml milk. Remove from the heat and leave to infuse for quarter of an hour then strain. Combine 2 egg yolks with 4oz/125g vanilla sugar in a heatproof bowl and whisk together till pale and moussey. Place the bowl over a panful of simmering water, cooking gently till the mixture coats the back of a spoon. Plunge the bowl in a basin of cold water, and leave to cool. Cover with cling film and place in the fridge.

Freeze in an ice cream maker for 15 mins, till the mixture has the consistency of whipped cream and then scrape into a plastic box and leave in the deep freeze for an hour. Remove from the freezer for 20 minutes before serving.

Instead of geranium or blackcurrant leaves, you could infuse a handful of rose petals, a few lavender sprigs or some angelica leaves in either the syrup (for a sorbet) or in the cream mixture if you prefer a more luxurious pud.

Unlike strawberries that need to be pureed first, whole raspberries freeze well, and can then be served as a treat at any feast or festival at any time of the year. We like them best combined with cream and gooey crushed meringue in a version of Eton Mess, which is traditionally served with fresh chopped strawberries.

I am not a jam maker. I rely on the excellent Mrs Honeyball, a lady of (I hope she will forgive me) mature years who has supplied The Kitchen Garden with jams for many seasons. She and her patiently courteous husband make jams, jellies

175

and pickles of every orchard, hedgerow and garden fruit known to man. Their year starts with six different marmalades and ends with cranberry preserve. Far be it from me to compete, though I do occasionally make fridge jam from the tiny amount of morello cherries to escape the blackbirds.

I simmer a few stoned cherries with a small piece of vanilla pod and an equal weight of sugar in a few spoonfuls of water, to prevent sticking. When the fruit is soft and the water absorbed, it is allowed to cool before being placed in an appropriately sized jam jar and kept in the fridge. I guarantee it will be eaten before it deteriorates. Italians add a few cherry stone kernels to give a Proustian amaretto flavour to the jam.

I met my husband in Milan, where he worked as a designer for Olivetti in Ettore Sottsass' studio and I was a fashion illustrator for a chain of smart department stores. We would head off to a villa on Lake Como at weekends and eat morello cherry jam with rolls and coffee for breakfast. Fond souvenirs of a very different world.

18th

The hottest day of the year (30 °C) found me, as spokesperson for the Henkeepers' Association, joining poultry enthusiasts, ministers, MPs and free range organic producers, at the House of Commons for the launch of a promising new initiative from Elm Farm Organic Research Centre, calling for a preventative vaccination policy. They are right – vaccination is the only socially acceptable solution to the prevention of avian flu in birds. I can't imagine the government thinks their culling policy will be a vote winner– the nation watches as millions of birds are slaughtered and family after family loses their pets to the men in white.

Nonetheless we are strange bedfellows – the poultry industry and the poultry enthusiasts. Millions of birds, in the hands of relatively few companies on the one hand, and we, the foot soldiers, numbering half a million, with a few birds each (but with substantially more votes) – on the other.

We have most in common with the free range organic producers because their welfare standards are much higher. It would be a tragedy to see commercial outdoor flocks lose the freedom we have all fought so hard to encourage, and to lose many of the rarer pure breeds. Struggling out through Westminster's corridors peopled by Babel's tourists, it's hard to imagine anything constructive emanates from this chaotic building, it's like a project designed jointly by Pugin, Faust and Walt Disney.

21st

Pick a few alchemilla strands and some spiky lavender, to bring the hot summer into the shady study and harvest the pretty flushed apricots, a little too early, just to save them from the birds. To my shame, I can't remember the variety, but it grows prolifically on the western border of the garden.

The flavour is quintessence of apricot, distilled through lack of rain, and only a few are needed to make a fragrant pudding poached lightly with vanilla and ground mace or rosewater, then blended with Greek yoghurt.

22nd

I think I made a good choice with the current Cockerel. He is quiet, gallant and calm. He looks after his ladies well, and although an enthusiastic lover, he is not promiscuous, unlike some of his predecessors.

Eggs produced by ladies under his regime are prolific and fertile, his offspring are growing well and his low volume crow is an extra advantage. And he is very handsome.

23rd

Another letter from Ben Bradshaw apologizing for his delay in replying to our last, but saying he has received an unprecedented number of letters, nearly four times the amount sent in 2005. Let's hope many are from groups supporting vaccination. At last, a feeling that Defra is beginning to understand our problems, and that practical bio-security solutions for free range birds, short of keeping them undercover with all its welfare complications which we want to avoid at all costs, are thin on the ground.

26th

Almost for the first time, I am begrudgingly grateful for the swimming pool. A project very dear to my husband's heart, he doggedly started digging the pool by hand, before the builders took over. Financed by the proceeds from an insurance claim due from a nasty car accident, I allowed myself to be convinced that a covered swimming pool was essential. Of course, the kids loved it, but then as time passed and they left home and my husband got involved in a greater passion, sailing, it has become a white elephant.

I still splash around most mornings during high summer, but my heart is not in it. I'm embarrassed by its *nouveau riche* connotations, it is unecological, and I begrudge the

money and time spent to maintain its high life existence. I would love to use the space as a studio, or gallery, but that would involve filling it in with sand to stop the sides collapsing, before flooring the void. Seems a little Draconian, and this month, it has been wonderful to wallow.

28th

A phone call from the Pensions Office. I have not filled in their labyrinthine form correctly. Judging by their calculations, if I ever give up work, I shall just about afford to live in a hut. Maybe that swimming pool building will be useful after all.

AUG*ust*

Harvest

Artichokes

A Fine Hen

Hollyhocks

Summer Storms

Scattered Feathers

Holidays

1st

You don't have to go *away* on holiday. It isn't compulsory to brave the airports and terrorist scares, to be disappointed with hotels, *gîtes* and villas, or to spend time among fellow travellers with whom you have nothing in common. You *are* allowed to stay at home, and take days out locally, go to good restaurants, treat yourself to special delights and spend money on yourself instead. Try it once, it can be very relaxing. Of course, it takes a little self control to loll about in a garden where you normally toil. Sometimes the weather here isn't bad either.

Nowadays, I only go away to visit friends. I'm a miserable wet blanket, I know, but because I travelled on my own from the age of six, terrified of missing connections and wearing a luggage label, I'm a reluctant traveller. Met by Universal Aunts and unreliable friends of my mother's, who'd obviously spent the taxi fare on other things, I was ferried across London on the underground, lugging huge school trunks full of undeclared duty free for my grandmother. I'm still shifty at customs.

10th

The drought has broken, not with a big splash, but with a drizzle. The stifling heat has dissipated, leaving fresher air. Since then it has rained steadily, in sheets. We have waited eight weeks for this water, but didn't expect it all to fall in two weeks. Amazingly, the grass and verges have turned from dull gold to lush green overnight. Giant storms have struck houses, tractors and burnt out whole fields. One poor man's oil tank was blitzed and the inferno destroyed a beautiful house he had just finished renovating. Another potential disaster to worry about. Please God, protect my oil tank.

As ever though, here in Suffolk, the weather is localised: one village's disastrous flood is another's welcome soak. The three month old chicks, now independent of mum, haven't really seen rain much before and standing as vertically as they can, they shelter in hopeless places. The best spots are reserved for older and wiser birds. They'll learn.

13th

Artichokes are my joy, my *plat de maison* and the Kitchen Garden's trademark. I plant them everywhere: in the vegetable plot, in large pots and in the borders. The most elegant and subtle of vegetables, their statuesque leaves and electric blue, bee-studded chokes - when left to flower, are outstanding. I overwinter my plants (var.'Vert de Laon' or 'Violetta di Chioggia') with a little straw under Thai bamboo cloches, intended to protect hens and chicks, but useful to keep away unwelcome diners and the frost from newly planted treasures. Artichokes grow well in an open soil and should be divided in March, so you never run short of plants. In their first year, discourage flowering to build up strength for future glories.

When my family were young, our favourite way to eat artichokes was simply to boil them in salted water till the base of the stem was tender to the fork. Then we sat *en famille* with a huge plate of artichokes and an even bigger platter for the mountainous debris. We would pick off the leaves one by one and dip them into a *vinaigrette*, pulling off the flesh with our teeth. When we got to the middle of the flower, the fluffy choke was discarded and the prized

186

heart mashed with dressing. Heaven. Nowadays, I tend to mash the hearts with softish hardboiled egg and mayonnaise. I have lost the patience to work my way into each heart. Maybe with grandchildren……..

Homemade mayonnaise bears little resemblance to its shop-bought relation.

Using an extravagant amount of oil (350mls) and 3 precious eggs - during the moult, eggs are hard come by, but it's worth every calorie. Bring all your ingredients from the fridge or larder to room temperature. Take a very clean bowl, three egg yolks, a pinch of salt and whisk. Add a few drops of olive oil. Carry on whisking and adding small drips till the mixture magically thickens.

Now you can add the rest of the oil in a steady stream. Finish with a squeeze of lemon juice. If you are in too much of a hurry and your mayo curdles, just add another yellow of egg and whisk again. Chopped tarragon or a dash of Dijon mustard will turn mayonnaise into a chef's signature dish.

If you have a little time, this recipe for artichokes filled with a soufflé mixture, is fairly stunning for a special supper.

Cook one large firm artichoke per person in boiling water with salt and lemon juice till tender (about 20 mins depending on size). Drain and scoop out the choke with a

189

spoon. Make a sauce to fill four artichokes by melting 3oz/80g butter, adding 3oz/80g flour and when it forms a ball, slowly add ¾ pint/450ml of milk, stirring vigorously till smooth. When cool add 3 egg yolks and some grated hard cheese to flavour. Fold in the firmly beaten egg whites a little at a time. Spoon the mixture into the artichoke nests. Bake for ¹/₂ hr till the soufflé has risen in a medium oven (400F/200C.)

If you are hard-hearted enough to harvest artichoke flowers when they are still in bud, pick now to marinade and preserve, so you can enjoy them later.

Trim 1lb/450g of precious buds into a bowl of water with the juice of a lemon, cutting off the stems, the outer layer of leaves and snipping the spines, and then boil till tender in salted water. Drain well and place in a large glass jar.

Reduce the marinade, uncovered in a saucepan combining one lemon, ½ pt/300ml water, 2fl.oz/50ml olive oil, thyme, bay leaves, a little chopped dried chilli, garlic cloves and peppercorns for about 15 mins. Gently pour over the artichokes, till well covered. Keep in the fridge once opened. Wash your hands well or the bitter taste of artichoke leaves will linger.

These hearts are particularly tasty on bruschetta.

Toast a couple of slices of bread, rub the surface with a cut garlic clove and drizzle with olive oil. Roughly mash a few hearts with a ripe chopped tomato and decorate with olives and capers. This Italian way of eating large slabs of country bread, turns an English sandwich into a Mediterranean feast, and works beautifully with tomatoes and mozzarella, grilled peppers and goats' cheese, baked aubergines and basil……….. The list goes on.

14th

Usually, the hens strut on, often perhaps a little disgracefully, until they drop, sometimes of heart attacks, but my oldest lady has decided to retire at the ripe old age of seven. A good age for an Orpington. The huge cocks only usually make five years, though average sized hens of other breeds will often live to at least 10 years of age. She has kept her distance from the rest of the flock, trying to set up residence in the scullery, and though of pink and perky *mein*, she won't eat and is definitely on the way out. I don't know how it will end, but, approaching, a significant birthday soon myself soon, we eye each other gloomily.

16th

The Very Old Hen has gone off, and Max eventually discovers her behind the pool building. She rallies a little, even eating a few sweetcorn kernels, but the next morning, I find her, stiff as a board.

A fine hen, mother of many, with nice feathering and compact shape – a eulogy I'd be proud of myself. I dig a deep hole in the rhubarb bed and bury her. This is a special place for the flock. All the hens hang out here to shelter under the enormous leaves and nibble them to lace. I'm sure the oxalic acid is an emetic and kills off any internal parasites. Her legacy will be increased vigour to the soil.

20th

Harvest, and for four days this cottage is blighted. Instantly, it seems we live on the hard shoulder of the M11, as combines, tractors and trailers hurl themselves along the narrow length of Church Lane. Under contract, the drivers are strangers, not bound by local knowledge of dog walkers, children on holiday and learner bike riders. They speed up and down, in a cloud of dust and chaff, desperate to keep to deadlines and squeeze every last penny out of their small profit margins, whatever the weather.

Long gone are the days when the village got involved. Both Troston farms have absentee landlords, one even lives abroad. A sign of the times. Bad times, when farmers don't have the interest of villagers at heart, the community doesn't care about the land and Harvest Festival is just a day when kids take tinned food to school.

Once they have disappeared in a rush of diesel fumes, the cat and I go for a walk over the stubble around the outside perimeter of our plot. Fascinating to see from the outside, the hedge we planted, now 15 foot high. A tapestry of wild greengage, blackthorn, hawthorn, yew, privet, and blackberry thicket, impenetrable and productive, a welcome relief from neighbouring barriers of Lawson's Cyprus.

In the vegetable plot, despite the lack of rain, the beetroot are ready to harvest.

So although the weather doesn't really warrant a refreshing cool soup, I pick three good roots and a handful of Swedish dill (sown just three weeks ago) a few cloves of fresh garlic and pop them in the pot, scrubbed and chopped and covered with stock. Simmered till tender and liquidized till smooth with a pinch of salt, 2 tablespoons of lemon juice, one of balsamic vinegar, and one of sugar, all dissolved and tasted (add more

sweet or sour to taste). Chill and serve with a dollop of crème fraîche and a sprinkle of dill.

For those who are not regular beetroot eaters, it's worth mentioning that this vegetable has a colourful effect on your pee.

Beetroot has a great affinity with raspberries, so a salad of beetroot, with a dressing made with raspberry vinegar is perfect. Make this delicious condiment using imperfect fruit, the last dregs of the early crop or late autumn berries.

Macerate one pint of mashed raspberries in a bowl, add half a pint of white wine vinegar, and cover. Stir every now and again for three days and then strain through muslin. Add sugar to taste and heat, without boiling for 10 minutes. Cool and bottle. Interestingly, if you substitute vodka for vinegar, you get an equally refreshing beverage!

23rd

To London for a stakeholders'meeting with Defra at Millbank. Nice to see our civil servants residing in such style. The poultry industry in all its variations – from the mega battery, broiler and free range representatives to the racing pigeon fanciers, caged bird keepers, turkey, duck and goose clubs, sitting with the tourist boards, the NFU, Game Conservancy, veterinary profession, (there are over 50 names on the stakeholders' list), all together to listen to Defra's Vaccination Policy.

Of course Defra still sticks to its policy NOT to vaccinate, but if it did, this is what it would do. And 10,000,000 doses of vaccine *have* been ordered – at between £2 and £20 per dose depending on the size of your flock. There won't be many takers in the industry, so maybe it is earmarked for us. We'd be prepared to pay £20 for each bird in our tiny flocks to be protected. I just hope the businessmen's lack of enthusiasm doesn't make Defra say that when offered vaccination, it was dismissed.

The dog days of August are always unreliable weather-wise – as I remember from many blighted birthday parties as a child, but here in town, I never notice the weather much, and stride off through the drizzle to tea with my cousin. With lovely cakes and champagne at the National Portrait Gallery café, we have a view over the rooftops of the Mall.

We had planned to meet in front of the Beckham Sleeping installation, in the Modern Icon section, where we felt either of us could lurk comfortably until the other arrived, but as the attendant informed me – Beckham's gone to York. So I hovered self consciously in the foyer till we eventually met up.

24th

Back home, the hollyhocks have reached the eaves. They grow so tall and vigorous and near the house, I worry maybe they are inextricably plumbed into our sewage system. Two eight foot stems have fallen in the wind, one a particularly good dark red and I shall dry the seeds to packet for my customers, to pass on their vigour. I prune the pyramid bay trees and collect the best leaves to put under the mat to dry between sheets of newspaper.

The hens are starting to moult. Feathers dot the lawn, trapped in spiders' webs, caught in hedges and blown by gales. My oldest surviving lady moulted her soft apricot feathers early, showing far too much *décolleté*, and was fashionably, if unattractively underdressed throughout the height of summer, not a pretty sight.

The Best Layer has gone into a dramatic moult, almost bald. Oven-ready she braves the cooler weather in a few strategically placed feathers. Loss of plumage is particular to each hen, they say the better the layer the heavier the moult, but moulting hens are bound to lay less, because all their protein goes into feather rather than eggs. And the cock is supposed to stop crowing and mating his wives. Fat chance.

The current cockerel is a judicious and quiescent bird. Unlike a previous incumbent, raised by a breeder as a subsidiary cock, who spent the first year of his life penned and watching the action in the main breeding cage from afar. Arriving here to six wives, he was in free range heaven, inevitably he over-egged the pudding. Elderly matrons, pullets, broodies and hens with chicks were romanced all too regularly, however frosty the reception.

A gentleman in every other respect, a season later, his ardour hadn't dampened. One old lady even dropped dead in *coitus*, the others spent their days, bare of back, stressed and off-lay, under the kitchen table. Unable to cope, just after Jean's death, a kind friend took him off on a sabbatical. Renamed Beau, cock a hoop, he was kept busy with fourteen new wives. Our ladies relaxed, skipping about in their new feathers, and the little black hen even started crowing. The following spring we hatched a bird who having risen through the ranks hen-pecked, respected the *status quo* - and we discovered the Orpington Saddle.

Stag turkeys have always massively towered over their hens and breeders have long protected their matrons with a leather saddle affair, designed to save their backs. Orpingtons have very soft feathers that are shed at the drop of a hat, and because of the disproportionate size of the cockerel, come springtime they are bald and often severely wounded.

Judicious blunting and filing of the cock's spurs and claws help, but then a breeder friend told me about her sister who made re-inforced canvas saddles, dyed an attractive buff colour and sized for an Orpington (as opposed to a massive turkey). We went into production. Now, many Orpington hens, nationwide, skip out carefree, confident in the knowledge that their flanks are protected from the ardours of the cockerel.

Last year, at one of our hen keeping courses, a customer brought out a photo of her hens decked out in homemade saddles - pretty as a picture in gingham and stripes and florals. Astounded, I muttered how attractive these jaunty ladies must be to their cockerel. Cockerel, she answered, what cockerel?

This is a perfect example of what my husband, a French Canadian, witheringly called the English illness, sentimentally wanting to humanize and dress up all animals in little jackets and aprons. I blame Beatrix Potter.

25th

A steady stream of visitors, and a renaissance of those wanting to take courses. Perhaps, because of the media's lack of interest, bird flu is just a dim memory. It's a hard line to tread, having to temper my natural enthusiasm with the warning this might not be the case.

The garden, though invigorated by the rain, is generally colourless, but the late summer gems are starting to flower and the low summer sun shows off these jewels in their best light. Enough to fill a vase with sparse offerings of nicotiana, dahlias and cosmos, stuck through a few sprigs of *Euphorbia wulfenii*.

The borage plants for sale in the yard have sprung back to life and the bees take courage from their nectar. Apparently borage stimulates the adrenalin gland, so it's the last thing this family needs, but the flowers are pretty in salads and can be cooked with sour fruits to reduce tartness, like angelica and sweet cicely. The leaves, of course are vital to Pimms and leafing through an old Booth's Handbook of Drinks, I remembered the classic version:

Pimms No 1 should apparently only have added to it: good quality fizzy lemonade, some ice, a slice of lemon, a little cucumber rind or borage leaves, when available. Their version also suggested an extra measure of gin, unsurprisingly.

Try it. A world away from the glass of fruit salad that passes for Pimms nowadays.

26th

Time to order bulbs to plant in pots to group outside the back door for season-long colour. A little thought now, will reward you richly throughout next year.

Pots of jaunty species Narcissi 'Sailboat' and 'Spring Dawn' in cream and pale yellow to lighten early spring months; bowls of bright, bright blue grape hyacinths Muscari latifolium and Iris reticulata 'Gordon' to flower in March/April; followed in May by buckets of pale greenish cream 'Spring Green' and darkest red 'Queen of the Night' tulips.

June heralds the statuesque Alliums – Christophii and firework-like Schubertii, and July boasts fragrant potted lilies: Madonna, Honey and Regale, if spared by the lily bugs. We finish the summer with a blaze of Agapanthus in large terracotta pots, that have been baking in a sunny spot, after a winter protected from the frosts. My favourites are the stunning navy blue Cherry Holley blooms and tiny delicate dwarf agapanthus.

Squirrel away hyacinth and narcissi bulbs for forcing in a cool, dry dark place until October, and keep your eyes peeled for unusual pots, seed boxes and other containers to set them off. Put garden bulbs aside for planting out in early autumn. I always feel unaccountably smug when I have ordered next year's bulbs. To be that far ahead of myself and in control is a rare and comforting feeling.

Here is a comprehensive sequential list of bulbs and corms to plant, so you'll have colour throughout the year, published by the Clare Bulb Company, who supply our outdoor bulbs:

Aconites	Hyacinth	Allium
Snowdrops	Narcissus	Lily tulip
Dwarf iris	Anemones	Camassia
Anemone blanda	Double tulip	Allium gig.
Species crocus	Frittilary	Lilies
Species tulips	Darwin tulip	Agapanthus
Muscari	Bluebell	Nerine
Dwarf Daffodils	Imperial lily	
Crocus	Dutch iris	
Daffodils	Parrot tulip	

27th

Bank holiday weekend. Off to a smallholding just outside Diss for a bank holiday fair. The indomitable Karen (who runs the excellent Samphire shop at Blickling Hall in Norfolk) has bravely opened her smallholding to the public for the first time and invited her shop's suppliers to show their wares. I'm included because she sells my books in great numbers.

Karen and her husband grow a huge variety of beautifully ranged vegetables and fruit, and keep pigs and goats, as well as very free range poultry in near utopian conditions. She sells her wares, and mine from the estate barn at one of the National Trusts most popular stately homes, including the most delicious ham I've ever tasted. I would be vegetarian if not for the produce of the pig. Good bacon and ham, raised humanely by hardworking smallholders like Karen, are my undoing.

So I load the car till we look like the Beverly Hillbillies – it would only take a few hens perched on top to complete the picture – and set off to spend the day in a tent, next to beekeepers, bakers, fudge-makers, brewers, growers and many interested punters.

To talk and sell solidly for a whole day, sandwiched between Herculean loading, unloading and driving, to say nothing of sampling much of the other stallholders' wares, is an exhausting, but rewarding day's work.

A snack before bed is all I need.

I grill a few slices of Karen's pigs' back bacon to wrap round a couple of fresh figs from a neighbour's tree. Yummy. Had the Rayburn been on, they would have tasted even better baked in an ovenproof dish in a hot oven for 10 minutes, but that won't happen for a while yet, I hope.

I'm a keen supporter of Farmer's Markets, having helped to set up our local weekly market five years ago. I wish others would take on the mantle and principles with more regular opening hours, so that decently farmed, locally and imaginatively sourced food were on sale to the public on a daily basis as a matter of course. Farm gate suppliers should get together and share the retailing on a co-operative basis, as they do on the continent. I wish Samphire was my local shop.

28th

Wedding Anniversary. It would have been our thirtieth. A lifetime past, a part of my life gone, but it looks as though I can function alone, and most of the time, I view the future with surprising optimism. Another milestone overcome and a chance to relax in a garden full of feathers. A still life depicting The Kitchen Garden at this time of the year, would show a feather, a lime key and some thistle down, trapped in a spider's web.

SEPT*ember*

1st

During the moult, the garden birds fall silent. The heatwave, followed by downpours has resulted in a mellow second Spring. The plants have summoned up the courage for a second flowering and the birds, now fully feathered again and chirruping, must be confused. This year's abundant harvest of hedgerow bounty – I have never seen blackberries like this – must tempt them to mate and nest.

2nd

The evening is so luxuriously warm that Max and I have supper in the garden. We light the outside oven. Much admired, this Portuguese terracotta beehive is incredibly thick and heavy, as Jean and the boys discovered when, like Atlas, they staggered to carry it from the drive to its place under the apple tree. In use, the door is closed on the red hot charcoal once the fire takes hold. It doesn't take long, but needs to be planned, so that there's enough time for the heat from the smouldering charcoal to cook our supper.

Max roasts a pan of peppers, tomatoes and courgettes, sliced lengthways. He spreads pesto on a slab of focaccia from the farmers' market, arranges the roast vegetable on top and then we grate parmesan over it at the table. We could probably cook supper for the entire village on the glowing embers, but as it turns chilly, we open the door and toast ourselves.

I grow pots of basil from April onwards, from seed in the conservatory or on warm window sills. Sowing at least six seedlings to an eight inch terracotta pot, which are always watered in the evening by wetting the soil, not the plant - or they'll wilt and rot off. There seem to be hundreds of varieties of basil: lemon, cinnamon, anise, lime, and spice, many of which are to be found in the excellent new Suffolk Herbs' catalogue.

I find the small-leaved Greek basil grows best for me, maybe the size of leaf makes it less susceptible to flop. The flavour is intense and pungent and livens up our delicate yellow courgettes, picked from plants that race across the spare ground in the asparagus bed, as well as being the perfect partner for tomatoes, peppers, beans, or anything that is ready to harvest now.

No taste is more redolent of the season than pesto. Before the last basil plants start to deteriorate, chop up as much pesto as you can to squirrel and store.

To make just 4oz of pesto, peel and slice four garlic cloves and put them in a food processor. I use my little Bamix hand held mixer. Add a large bunch of basil excluding the thickest stems, 1½ oz/40g of pine nuts, some salt and pepper and slacken with 3-4 tablespoons of good olive oil.

I prefer my pesto quite roughly chopped, so I stop processing before it turns into a smooth paste. Sprinkle with grated Parmesan or Pecorino. It is possible to substitute almonds or walnuts for pine nuts, and coriander and parsley for basil, but nothing beats a classic pesto.

Spread it onto lamb cutlets, tuna steaks or even chicken breasts if you must. We love to smear it thickly on pizza,

212

topped with sliced ripe peppers (red or orange, not the unripe green ones) with shavings of parmesan; on pasta – obviously; in risotto (added to the rice at the last minute, because heat causes the pesto to loose its vibrant colour); on sliced beefsteak tomatoes, layered between goat's cheese and beetroot, or swirled into a minestrone or this deliciously simple yellow courgette soup.

Fry a few courgettes, leeks and a little garlic till soft in some butter. Add a pint of stock, a big bunch of basil, season and simmer for a quarter of an hour. Add the juice of a lemon, ½ pint of single cream, serve with a small bowl of pesto to spoon in or serve chilled, topped with extra chopped basil.

3rd

A bad day. Shirley 'from up the road' brought me a mammoth basket of greengages a few days ago. I have stuffed myself with as many as is humanly possible without exploding and now, in a panic with lots of other things to do, set out to turn the rest into compote, before they beat me to it and turn into compost. Unable to concentrate, and overcome with grumpiness at my inability to put the greengages and their stones into their appropriate containers, I stomp off, get involved in something else, and forget the fruit on the stove. The smell – the ruined saucepan – the waste. Is this the future? I go to bed.

4th

Wake up feeling better. I am always optimistic in the mornings. Set off on a marathon sloe picking trek. Start in the garden, some of our own blackthorn bushes are prolific.

215

The navy blue berries with their frosty bloom are pretty enough to spare a space, but the bushes sucker dreadfully, so I've relegated them to the peripheral hedgerow.

Then I wend my way picking, up the lane. Folklore dictates we should wait till after the first frost to pick sloes, but by then they've fallen or been eaten by the birds, and anyway, we can replicate the cold snap by popping them into the freezer for a few weeks. A phone call from someone offering damsons, so we'll have damson as well as sloe gin in the shop this Christmas.

5th

To Helions Bumpstead in Essex, to set out my wares again, this time as shopping relief to the ladies who lunch in aid of the Museum of Garden History. Not perhaps the most pressing of causes, but run by a jolly crowd, held in an exquisite garden, and this year there's the chance to hear Anna Pavord talk and ask the question Why Garden?

She spoke brilliantly, with knowledge and enthusiasm, giving her main reasons for gardening as the desire to create something of beauty and show it off, to nurture plants, perhaps to collect them, to provide a wildlife haven, to grow food, and to exercise some control over at least one element in one's lives, all very salient points. She added another reason, not paramount, but still important in my case – for profit. It has been crucial for me to earn my living and without my garden as venue and inspiration, the spectre of the supermarket check-out loomed.

7th

Now that the summer holidays are over, it's time to take stock in the chicken run. Five years ago, we definitely did have stock. We hatched out more chicks than usual due to a hidden broody who managed to hoodwink me and produce nine chicks. Accidents happen, even in the best chicken runs. All survived, thanks to the expert ministrations of mum and surprise, surprise…the old Cockerel – aka Casanova – born again briefly as a New Man.

We looked out on Victorian nursery book scenes of farmyard idylls with cock, hen and chicks happily scratching in the meadow. Inevitably there was a downside, guess how many took after their dad? Would you believe, six were cockerels and just three were pullets. So we sent out a message on the website: wanted, good free range homes with at least six hens for Orpington cockerels of impeccable pedigree and all the right instincts. We homed three with families, kept one to replace the old boy, by then nearly five years old and sadly reaching his sell-by-date and the remaining two went to reliable breeders, keen to get that Kitchen Garden bloodline.

This year we have hatched three hens. Alleluia.

When your chicks reach the age of twelve weeks, it is possible to tell their sex. If you take a piece of card and slide it under the neck or shoulder plumage, the henny feathers will be rounded at their tip, while the young cockerel's will be pointy. It is not an exact science.

Earlier in the year, Hugh Burton, whose mother Pauline breeds Orpingtons (so he should know better) was helping at one of our courses, when he spotted the Beauty's two chicks in the garden. To the attending students, he pointed them out as a classic example of a young pullet and a young cockerel. My spirits plummeted, to drop even further at the next course when we both agreed they were probably two cockerels after all.

Now we know for certain that they are two beautiful hens, large, round, but definitely female.

As pullets, they're at a loose end, tagging on to the main flock, but left on the peripheries. For virtually the only time in their lives, they can fly, or at least flutter. Later, it will take jet propulsion to achieve lift-off. Very friendly to humans, and intensely curious, the two sisters have taken to coming into the kitchen and sitting on the mat next to the Rayburn. All my hens love to come into the house, and if it weren't for Max, who shoos them out instantly and the spectre of Health and Safety, we'd probably all be sitting round the kitchen table together now.

9th

Nigel has cut 'the meadow'. So it's my exhausting task to rake all the 'hay' into stacks. I make a huge pile every year and as the pile rots, the plants underneath die, leaving a neat bed to plant up with new wild flowers. A much easier way than trying to insert young plants into the matted substrata.

This year I want to plant teasels to supply food for the goldfinches. I found a heartbreakingly beautiful nest, a tiny thimble made of thistledown, feathers and lichen. I try to leave all seed heads standing to sustain the birds in the garden over winter, except those that I need for decorations, like the cardoons, alliums, Chinese lanterns and honesty seeds, or those that are too prolific and getting out of hand. Even the fussiest of gardeners can let their hens into the

garden at this time of the year. Birds are good at balancing their own nutritional needs and will find all sorts of nourishing snacks among the leftover fruit, seeds, weeds and garden pests. Elder, hawthorn and blackberries are particularly nutritious, and I've noticed the comfrey leaves get well nibbled.

My flock have become so blasé about apples, they will only eat the pips – once the fruit degenerates into a pureé, and I think the ducks wait till the mixture ferments.

I read with interest the other day in the industrial poultry press, that the Plume Poppy *Macleaya cordata* apparently holds the key to increased weight gain and resilience to infection. Since this is a plant that grows unpecked to 6ft here, it's obviously a delicacy that has escaped my flock's beady eyes.

Short grass is a good source of protein and I grow extra rows of spinach and beet specially to give them the greenery to produce those wonderful yellow yolks. Be warned though, too much greenery can have a dramatic effect on droppings.

As far as I can tell though, hens have the sense not to eat poisonous plants. Here, they forgo yew, laburnum, foxgloves and monkshood, and obviously we don't use chemical weedkillers or slug pellets. Nor do we have many slugs, come to think of it, thanks to the ducks.

221

10th

Jacques birthday in New Zealand. Cheer myself up with a long Skype chat. They won't be back till Christmas. It seems a lifetime since they left. Even my boarding school training of wishing time away seems inadequate. Co-incidentally, a visit from L, a fellow convent girl from Thildonck, an Ursuline nunnery in Belgium. She was number 352 to my 353. We hadn't met for about half a century, but her memory was worryingly far sharper than mine. Perhaps her souvenirs of that huge, depressing, rather cruelly authoritarian place were pleasanter.

I remember being timid and overwhelmed by the routine, religion and foreignness of the place, where I was sent at the age of 9, unable to say anything more than *pomme* and *pomme-de-terre* (not a vocabulary that gets you far in life) but needless to say, by the end of the first term I could speak French fluently, albeit with *l'accent Belge*, which has since been superceded by Quebecois, but she remembers me as being arty and rebellious…..

15th

Today, Nigel comes to give the yew hedges their annual haircut, shaving this year's growth. An expert, like Edward Scissorhands, he shears and shapes, neatening the vista, and tapering heights, so that the avenue looks longer than it actually is. A false perspective, a little horticultural joke. Not very funny though, without his help. This hedge reached maturity about 12 years after planting, despite several years of drought.

The trenches for the 12inch tall bare-rooted plants were dug 20 odd years ago by an old boy from the village, so deep and wide we felt he may well have had experience in the First World War. They were then filled with all the compost

222

from the bins, much of it unrotted, old turves, anything he could get hold of before planting. I wish now, I'd installed a leaky pipe. People forget that hedges need feeding and watering and just leave them to get on with it.

The clippings are bagged up and used to go, via an agency, to pharmaceutical companies to make anti-cancer drugs from the taxol present in yew leaves, but this year we were unable to find a home for them, so it's off to the municipal tip.

A Harvest Moon

20th

Just back this morning from a flying visit to my friends the Greys in Lewes. Back to the remains of a woodpigeon in the study, the cat's unfinished meal, her protest at being left alone; a pile of mail – lots of cheques for the duck book that has had a small mention in a magazine, and there, among the 435 spam messages, is an email from Defra, accepting my invitation to lunch. How many civil servants can I accommodate, where is Troston and should they wear protective clothing?

I reply six, near Bury St Edmunds and, no, since they will only be visiting one holding, the white suits won't be necessary. I hope I don't live to regret this visit, but I really feel there is no understanding of our situation. Inevitably Defra's experience is of battery units, housing tens of thousands of birds in strict bio-security; or of broiler huts full of young pullets fed so fast they can't carry their own weight, on food so full of fat and protein that their meat is no longer a low fat option.

My Orpingtons, a breed that grows as big as a chicken can under normal conditions, can be held in a cupped hand at six weeks, the age of a supermarket carcass.

I'm not surprised that these perfectly charming, well-educated people find it hard to understand why there is a large tranche of the poultry-keeping community, who has decided to keep these same sad creatures as pets and give them free range in gardens to live long and natural lives.

An interesting message from the agent of a friend of mine, writer Elspeth Thompson, whose lovely columns in The Guardian and The Independant have always been a favourite read. She has a publishing proposition for something very like this book, or at this stage, this virtual book – 75% of which is still either in my head or in scruffy notebooks.

I have always published my own books. There are nine, so far. Not exactly a Murdochian feat, but I reckon over the last decade we've sold 60,000 or so. But I have been struggling a little with the scale of this one, not just the number of pages, but the design – I miss Jean's graphic and computer skills, and also an overview, an editor's eye.

This vanity press business can result in some bloomers. I could end up with egg on my face. The clincher may be funds. I'll have to sell a lot of books to finance the printing. Bird flu and Max's college fees have put pay to the sort of profits I might have been able to draw on. But I am used to having my own way, especially on the way a book looks

and feels. Can I compromise? It may all be pie in the sky, but it's worth a thought.

Race off into the vegetable garden to harvest some veg for supper – yellow dwarf beans and courgettes 'Meraviglia di Venezia' and 'Gold Rush', beetroot 'Bulls Blood', Japanese onions, wild rocket and chervil are ready to pick. Not a cohesive menu, but very pretty.

Get stuck in to a little light weeding and deep thought. Before long the hens join in and I'm lost. Dusk, and then I look down. Too late, still in my town clothes, yet another pair of decent shoes written off, and on the way in I catch my vintage Missoni on a thorn - the worse for wear, struck off the best dressed list, again.

21st

I have been to the Greys to help them organize a system for their ducks. They have always been my duck mentors. I keep mine in totally the wrong way, encouraging semi wild birds to breed prolifically by over feeding – or so I'm told. Sue and John, on the other hand have always been exemplary duck keepers.

Sadly, their little flock has been decimated by the urban fox. Their drake, the legendary Declan, half Campbell, half-Mallard (the wrong half Mallard of course) and his poor put-upon ladies have supplied the Grey family with eggs and amusement for ten years, until several vixen strikes dispatched the entire flock.

227

They want to start again, so we have designed a run, with electrical re-inforcement and a wire apron for times when no-one's at home. The real design brief is to make it look attractive and unlike the avian Colditz it actually is. We've decided to front the wire with picket fencing painted in Farrow and Ball Drab and make it adaptable to Defra regs, should they have to keep the new flock under cover. I do a drawing, helped by the cat, who is always extremely friendly after we've been away and wants to sit on my lap.

En route, we visited A, who lived opposite us in London and baby sat for Jacques and Max. She now has two beautiful daughters of her own, who keep two hens of undecipherable lineage in their tiny back garden, in an Eglu, the new henhouse and run from the boys at Omlet. This is the ideal solution for this situation. The children adore their hens, who lay an egg a day each and live safely in their desirable state of the art accommodation, coming out into the main garden whenever the family is at home.

26th

Time to dismantle the compost heaps, so that the hens can sort through for pests and future frosts will help break down the contents. There are many differing horticultural philosophies on the subject of compost making. I favour the longterm/leave it to rot system, with layered imput from kitchen, garden, mower and henhouse. All allowed to mascerate on their own for at least a year, sometimes longer, with the ingredients heated up by grass cuttings and accelerated by chicken manure. But we have the space for a dozen or so heaps, each at different stages of decomposition.

They say the best compost is made of cut vegetation and corrugated brown cardboard, moistened with human pee. Chicken run debris – straw, newspaper, feathers and dropping is pretty potent stuff too, being high in both nitrogen and phosphates.

Commercially farmed poultry manure is too strong and will burn plants, if mulched directly. It should be left to rot down, but droppings from garden birds, fed a more varied, lower protein diet can be used immediately, especially on greedy fruit like currants. So organize a holiday for your hens in the fruit cage come early winter.

Most of the droppings around the garden make their own way into the soil, or are dug in. Some are swept up from paths or terraces with leaves, and others are mown up when the grass is cut. All go onto the compost heap, naturally layered with bedding and whatever else is gardened.

Particular care should be taken to prevent rats from dining on the kitchen content, so I make sure the hens polish off most of the really tasty eatables first. Amazingly, I still find bits of Action Man's kit in the soil and digging in the beds. Obviously, in times past, he used to frolic among the vegetables.

Other *objets trouvés* include gloves, kitchen knives and last year, a pair of Felco secateurs, that Keith miraculously managed to recondition and are now in use on a daily basis.

I find dismantling the heaps to be the most exhausting chore in the garden. My Pilates teacher recently dismissed gardening as proper exercise, but I challenge her to a solid day's lifting and bending, sorting and sieving, distributing and broadcasting, maybe followed by a little hearty raking. Perhaps her definition of gardening ends at deadheading, gentle weeding or swanning about giving orders to staff.

The local council collects household rubbish on a fortnightly basis. We've been given three bins to fill. A blue one for recyclable plastic and paper;

a brown one for plant matter (in our case mostly woody bits too large to compost small scale, but too insubstantial as fuel for the wood burning stove); and a black bin for non-recycled stuff, including food, spent batteries, aerosols, fruit juice cartons and pottery. On a good week, the latter is almost empty.

Glass bottles find a home in the skip in the pub car park, old clothes go to the jumble and occasionally we take part in village car boot or garage sales. It's a time consuming business, disposing of rubbish.

28th

Nice visit from the Editor and her deputy from The English Garden Magazine. An article on us in their excellent publication in July resulted in a lot of their readers visiting this garden. So they have decided they would like a monthly column on growing and cooking vegetables fruits, herbs etc and even a little corner about keeping hens.

Am thrilled to be writing on subjects I really love and, having done most of the work involved, for this book already, it should be fun. Useful that Sara has already photographed the garden for a year, which means we don't have to wait too long to publish. It will be good to have a regular income. I already write a monthly column for the Smallholder magazine, but that's for love (at 5p a word, it's hardly for money).

30th

The Kitchen Garden closes to visitors at the end of September. A worthwhile season, with amazing extremes of weather that only this country could produce.

OCT*ober*

Walnuts

Old Friends

Damson Gin

New Feathers

Potted Bulbs

Pumpkins & Squashes

Apples, Pears and Quinces

1st

I always feel invigorated by October. The bright days fill me with optimism. From childhood, the start of the school year with its seasonal change of classroom and change of clothes and a visit to Daniel Neals, the outfitters, in Bournemouth, was a time of great energy. It seems much more apt to celebrate the New Year now than during the cold dark days of January. There must be a sect somewhere that celebrates its genesis in October. I would join. The intensity of keen autumn days galvanizes the spirit, energizes, recharges the batteries, and increases the serotonin levels.

2nd

To Oxford, by Stagecoach, paying just £8 return, to lurch across country, through places I'd never visited before, like Milton Keynes and Bedford, in order to celebrate the 60th birthday of Jane, my best friend from school. A surprise congratulatory lunch with many familiar faces from my early teens and then a punt trip down the river.

Looking round the other guests, we are mostly single women, all of a similar age – talented, intelligent, attractive women of wit and appetite – coping with life alone, apparently with enthusiasm and efficiency. Where are our partners? Embarked on separate journeys with second families probably, in midlife crisis, or dead? Men of this generation don't survive alone with the same panache.

3rd

Back home. Watch as three skeins of geese come in to the water meadows nearby. Their cries reminding me with dread of the returning possibility of

disease. What will this year's migration bring? It is almost a year since the first inklings of the horror of avian influenza in Europe were jumped on by the media, following the finding of virus in Turkish and Rumanian poultry.

In Troston, the local farm picked this moment to decide to open a 'free range' unit and abattoir right in the middle of the village, blighting many houses. The absentee owner was petitioned, and a Parish Council meeting was called, chaired I'm told, by a surprisingly biased vicar, where the so-called independent vet turned out to be employed by the poultry company, and the majority view was railroaded.

A year on, the unit has enlarged, but the farm has applied for planning permission to build over 50 executive houses on the site, citing local opposition to farming within the village as the reason they can no longer survive without selling land to property developers. So much for democracy. Where will the possible hundred extra children go to school and how will these tiny single lane roads cope with an extra hundred cars? We've suggested 20 houses, five of which to be affordable and available to local people only. But this is not a tempting proposition to a property developer.

A late brood of ducklings from the black duck with a white bib, who reminds me of a mother superior, now with a row of tiny nuns. I wonder how many will survive. It will depend on the weather. The flock will keep coming to the garden until the windfall apples have rotted, and then they will all disappear to the pond over the road, as they have

done for half a century, paying us a flying visit morning and evening to be fed on the hard standing in front of the garages.

4th

Visit from Defra policy makers. At an earlier Stakeholder's meeting, I'd casually invited them to see how garden henkeepers actually keep their birds. As arguably the largest group of keepers, with admittedly the smallest number of birds, we are probably the largest group of voters, so presumably our reaction to a massive cull of pet birds would be of interest to the Government. So it was with some trepidation, that today I welcomed Defra's Communications Manager, their Policy Advisor from the Exotic Disease Prevention Team (who advises on vaccination issues) and three members of the Health Planning team. White suits were eschewed because this site was the delegation's only visit.

I was keen to point out how we differed from most keepers: we don't breed for sale, show our birds or even sell our produce much; our hens rarely leave the premises, and since we encourage home breeding, our flock content is fairly static. Obviously, we are deeply attached to our birds, so the welfare issues involved in keeping hens used to ranging free, undercover - in the event of A I were stressed. As were worries about the likely disappearance of commercial free range flocks and the rarer pure breeds.

Conversation at lunch was slightly stilted. The egg salad, designed to show off the rich yellow yolks of truly free range hens, wasn't greeted with huge enthusiasm - Defra's healthy eating policy has obviously yet to be developed (judging by the plates of sandwiches and crisps we're always offered at Millbank) but the blackberry and apple crumble was wolfed down. Subsequent requests for the topping recipe (porridge oats, walnuts, brown sugar and walnut oil) have been answered and emailed.

On their side, Defra wanted to find out how best to communicate with people like us; how their principles could work on smaller premises and what practical problems would arise if they were ever to decide to allow vaccination. They promised to include the Henkeepers' Association in decisions that concern us, even though our tiny flocks are probably in the lowest risk category. They had the grace to admit they had no idea anyone kept hens in this way and that the visit had been an education.

My flock of Orpingtons handled the visit with aplomb and included an impromptu exhibition of mating behaviour in larger poultry breeds!

5th

Swept up the leaves under the walnut tree, not just to keep the lawn tidy, but to stop the rotting leaves and nut cases killing the grass. A bit of a chore, but beneficial both for the waistline and as energetic heart massage. In bending down to pick up the leaves, the bonus is inhaling that heavenly smell. Trying to bottle that aroma a few years ago, we made Brou – a walnut liqueur from Jane Grigson's 'Good Things'.

Cramming a jar in July with the unripe green nuts, we topped up with brandy, sugar to taste and a cinnamon stick. The nuts were strained out after three months, and the liqueur left to mature. Two years later, I have a small glass here at my elbow, as I type. To be honest, it is slightly disappointing, it doesn't capture that slightly medicinal smell, more cough mixture than elixir, but it does grow on you.........

The squirrels are determined to bury the entire crop of nuts anywhere. In the Spring, seedlings pop up everywhere in the lawn. If left to sprout we would have groves of walnut trees. Each of my newly planted pots of bulbs will contain at least half a dozen nuts each, buried treasure and winter feasts hidden in forgotten hideaways. Rooks also enjoy the odd walnut, regularly managing to strip most of my friend Barbara's trees.

6th

A jolly evening spent bottling all the sloes and damsons that have passed their week's quarantine in bags in the freezer and now need to be stored in huge old pickle jars.

Fill up your container to nearly halfway ($^3/_8$) with fruit, add an eighth of sugar (I like my gin quite dry) and then soak the berries right up to the top with gin. Add a couple of cinnamon sticks. Other recipes suggest proportions of a third fruit to a third alcohol sweetened with a third sugar, which I find a little too sweet. The jars are left on the kitchen shelf and the fruit is stirred every other day.

7th

This year's pumpkins were a disaster. Not enough rain early on and then too much and they rotted. Others must have got their timing right so I buy a huge orange pumpkin at the farm gate in Barton, more as decoration than food. Pumpkin is overrated, I feel. I'm not fond of it sweet, and as a savoury it depends on heavy spicing. In this pumpkin and tomato chutney though, from Penny Hands, it acts as a carrier for some good flavours.

For 3 large jars, peel and de-seed 2¼lbs/1kilo of cubed pumpkin and skin and slice 1lb 2oz/500g of ripe tomatoes. Peel and slice 2 onions and 2 cloves of garlic. Put in a preserving pan with 2 tablespoons sultanas, 1lb 10oz/750g soft dark sugar, 1 tsp salt and 2 tsp each of ground ginger, black peppercorns and allspice. Add 1¼pt/750ml good cider vinegar and boil, till soft and jammy, stirring to stop the mixture sticking. Ladle into sterile jars and keep for a few weeks before opening.

10th

The weather turns and the first storms cause the walnuts to drop *en masse*. 7 o'clock, (the cock crows first at 6.55am) I skirt round the tree in the dim, misty light to harvest what the squirrels have left me. Mostly the nuts come away from their felty green outer shells as they fall, if not a sharp kick/squash with a boot will do the trick. Best not to use your hands, the skins stain, and if they get under your fingernails, no amount of scrubbing will clean them. An orange stick dipped in a little diluted bleach works if you really have to look tidy.

I crack a few nuts and share them with the Cockerel. He loves them, but strangely the hens don't. The kernels are still slightly wet, but milky and flavourful, though the inner membrane is bitter and needs to be peeled off, making

eating them a lengthy rigmarole. Best to stack most of them somewhere cool to dry in cardboard supermarket tomato boxes. It's my mission to collect several times a day - to beat the pesky squirrels. My jacket pockets are constantly bulging with walnuts. I must take care not to enter dotty old woman territory.

I sometimes catch sight of my reflection in the French windows, and wonder what my mother's doing here, wearing that coat of mine?

14th

The redoubtable Mr.Ellis, patron of the clan Ellis, whose practical family are spread throughout the area, pays us a timely visit to turn on and service the Rayburn, auguring the change of the seasons in a welcome and tangible way. My faithful black Rayburn, pumping out background heat.

When it gets really cold, we'll light our hungry woodburner and outside the smell of woodsmoke will curl in and out of the lime trees. Inside smells are always better when the air is warm. This is friendly heat, a heat to sit by. A cleverly designed stove, made by a hippy metal worker friend with doors that open on one side of the chimney to the sitting room, and on the other to the kitchen.

In the past, dealing with the fire was my husband's territory, but now I have her tamed, she usually works a treat, gobbling up all our bits of waste wood from the garden.

Phone my friend Madeleine in Le Marche in Italy. A recent exile, I went to visit her last year at this time, perched in her hilltop farmhouse, surrounded by orchards of luscious figs, medlars, pomegranates, almonds and persimmons.

NB Italians eat persimmons, (sometimes sold here in supermarkets as Sharon Fruit – what a good choice of name) as a pudding, with the top removed and whisky poured inside.

She is happy, but wants me to send her some Euphorbia *wulfenii* seedlings! Unlike many of my friends, I'm not tempted by voluntary expatriation, however tempting the venue. I sampled all those delights in my youth, and now need the security of familiar people and landscapes. One or two of the intrepid travellers are straggling back again, *la dolce vita* and *la vie en rose* are not quite what they'd expected. Still, with global warming, perhaps we'll soon be growing exotic fare like persimmons too. Kew are planting olive trees…

15th

In the chicken run, the annual moult is nearly over and some of my older ladies are looking a trifle disreputable. Despite having spent the last month doing little other than preen their new feathers, it seems they've paid scant attention to that last important part of their anatomy – the *derrière*. So, today, a bright autumn day, one by one I've caught them, protesting.

Taking off their saddles (because at last, the Cockerel has lost interest), I'm sitting on a straw bale, next to a basin of warm soapy water (bubbles courtesy of Baby Bath). Clad in a waterproof apron and a pair of marigolds, with hen in lap, I've cleaned up their bums, sponging, and where necessary snipping and finishing and – for those with unwelcome guests - a quick puff of anti-mite spray from the pet shop.

Scratching slightly, I've had a shower myself and now my girls are parading the orchard in their new finery, the indignity of their forced wash and brush-up, a fading memory.

The swimming pool has turned emerald green and slimy. The late good weather has extended the season to the last possible minute, but Max will remedy with his armoury of dreaded chemicals and then put the pool to bed. Re-enrol at the local gym to join the ladies at the aqua-aerobic class. Fortunately, the innate silliness of our synchronised jogging (to opera with a disco beat, music from hell) is hidden underwater and it's excellent exercise. The water adds extra buoyancy and scope to our range of athleticism and protects our aging joints.

16th

To Mother's in Sandbanks in Dorset to celebrate her birthday. My memories of the area as a teenager at my second boarding school, (this one subsidising C of E vicar's daughters – no-one can say I didn't have a broad education) are of sandy paths, pine trees, rhododendron bushes and beach shacks.

The school had a changing hut where we swam, on a huge plot right on the isthmus, which now houses the most expensive real estate in the world, on a par with Manhattan. Nowadays it's a haven of tasteless white shiny blocks of flats - architectural exercises in how to fit the most verandahs on one building.

Ended a difficult day, sitting in my mother's flat, wrapped in her old mink stole, currently used as a draught excluder, because the central heating went off hours ago. Max and I watched Four Weddings and a Funeral for the enth time and finished off the Veuve Clicquot we had brought along to celebrate.

20th

Planted the garlic 'Rosso di Sulmona' a red variety to be harvested next year from midsummer onwards. Demolished one of the leaf mould heaps, helped by the hens. A first class soil conditioner, as well as tasty snack for poultry it seems, I've saved some for the first layer to fill the bulb containers.

Planting bulbs in pots is like cooking: first install a layer of crocks, then one of leaf mould, then a sprinkle of grit. Pack in your bulbs and top off with compost and a final layer of grit to deter beetles. Label and hide away from the mice and squirrels, in a spot sheltered from the rain. Will plant the rest of the tulips in the cutflower plot later in November. One of the leaf mould bays is now ready and waiting to be replenished with fallen leaves, reluctant this year to leave their branches.

Move the orchids and potted tarragon inside, to the shelter of the conservatory. Bring in the last few vines from the tomatoes to the fruit bowl to ripen inside. Amazing late crop of raspberries, but their flavour lacks sunshine. So I've added them in a jar, to the contents of a bottle of mead,

which has spent sometime in the larder. Will report later. Smells divine.

Update, it was undrinkable and nearly exploded. Do not try this at home.

A welcome present of a box of pears. Everyone wanders round with bags of fruit at this time of the year, but I can't even give away my apples, everyone has them already. I shall have to buy a juicer. I say this every year, then because my tree is a biennial cropper, next year we'll have none, and by the following year I'll have forgotten the waste.

Save a few precious pears to grate on my porridge for breakfast, and then bake the rest in a dish in wine with vanilla pods and a grating of nutmeg. Add a sliced quince as an afterthought.

Generally, I'm not fond of combining sweet and savoury elements in dishes, my meal from hell would involve sweet and sour anything, but pears have always had an affinity with cheese, so for lunch I slice a pear in an autumn salad, combined with a few of our walnuts and a slice of dolcelatte, crumbled on a bed of watercress.

Almost need take out a mortgage to buy a new pair of Irish Dubarry boots. My last pair has stylishly warmed my toes, curing my chilblains to boot, for these last ten years, but now MUST be relegated to the garden only. The shiny new pair is comfortable, waterproof and will be virtually my only footwear from now until April, apart from the odd sortie in smarter footwear in the evening.

21st

Walking briskly up the lane early this foggy morning, I disturb hares and pheasants that scatter before my lumbering form. Then larger shapes loom out of the mist, springing off in different directions, a small herd of roe deer. I always feel privileged to glimpse these wild survivors from another age and wonder how long will they continue to thrive in this changing landscape?

A Hunter's Moon.

25th

I love leaves. Obviously when they're green on the tree, but even when they have fallen. Most of all, I love their iconic shapes and their brilliant colours, and I enjoy making leaf mould. Why do people moan about fallen leaves in their gardens. Don't waste them, turn them into leaf mould. It's a luxury plant food. Oak, birch, beech and hawthorn - the smaller leaves are best. Others are best shredded first and then stacked in wired compost bays. Add the odd layer of grass cuttings in the spring and by next autumn, you'll have a wondrous soil conditioner, and empty bins, ready to take next years' fallen leaves.

Drop round to see my god-daughter Charlotte. Her family's garden is usually rich pickings for wonderful leaves, seed heads and berries. The previous owners had been inimitable plantsmen, and the garden has now been successfully modernised and minimalised. It looked glorious, but the colours haven't turned. Leaf colour is determined by reducing daylight hours, not by temperature. This year it will be very late, so I'll have to wait to collect my usual cache of goodies. Hope there'll be time for them to dry out before the Christmas Decoration Course we're holding for a magazine's readers next month.

28th

The clocks change. Why? I can never understand who benefits from lighter early mornings. Even in the country, most outdoor workers would welcome a longer and safer afternoon. It takes the hens and I forever to adjust to the new timetable.

In the garden the cosmos is still flowering, so are the hellebores, old-fashioned roses and violets, and my favourite pinky-beige auricula, that performed so prettily in April, has put on a valiant autumn show, though a mere shadow of its Easter outing. Will it re-appear next year or be exhausted by this year's double effort?

29th

To the Car Boot Sale at Woolpit. *Le tout* Suffolk, still stalwart in their summer finery on this beautiful Sunday, with their dogs, out to catch the bargains. Everything from 'tame doves at £1.50' to a Pirelli rubber boat; from a heavy metal fireback depicting a Springer with a bird in its mouth to a full size teepee, each very tempting in its own particular way. But I forgo those attractions in favour of some good old galvanized ware, a pine writing box, a set of cookie jars, some pots and various other odds and ends to sell at Christmas. Had I been looking for plastic toys or childrens' clothes, the choice would have been overwhelming. A great way to re-cycle though.

Spend the rest of the day messing around cheerily with quinces. My tree *Cydonia oblongata* 'Champion' with its silvery leaves and white cupped flowers, is the prettiest tree in the garden. If I had the space I'd plant 'Meech's Prolific' and 'Portugal' with its almost orange fruit. I've always thought quinces would have been a more convincing temptation for Eve in the Garden of Eden. That uplifting ochre, and the perfume - probably my favourite garden smell, I always leave a few in my blue bowl, and there they rot, convincingly evoking All Hallow's Eve.

Decide to bottle some Spiced Quinces to eat with the goose on Christmas Day.

Peel, quarter and core about 5lb/2.25kg of quinces. My 'Champion' has quite soft flesh, but if your tree produces rock hard boulders, it is easier to poach or bake them whole in the oven before attempting to chop them.

Simmer the fruit slowly for about 20 minutes with a pint/600ml of white wine vinegar, 1lb/450g of muscovado sugar, a cinnamon stick, a finger of chopped ginger, a few thin strips of lemon peel and a tablespoon each of black peppercorns and cloves.

Leave the mixture overnight to macerate, then carefully strain off the liquid, keeping the spices to one side and divide the fruit into preserving jars. Reduce the syrup in a pan at a rolling boil till thick, but take care not to let it burn.

Strain the liquid again and pour over the quinces, distributing the spices and lemon peel between the jars. This preserve improves with keeping, so move one jar to the back of the larder for next year.

Easier to make is Quince Ratafia.

Grate or chop the quinces and place in a large wide necked jar, so that the final ratio is 1/3 quince to 1/3 spiced sugar and top up with vodka. Leave for a couple of months, then strain and drink this ruby infusion to toast the New Year. It's worth saving a few late quinces in a cold store to stuff your Christmas bird.

NOV*ember*

Pullet's Eggs

Warming Soups

Autumn Leaves

Wreaths

Department Stores

Unwelcome Visitors

Prodigal Sons

1st

Bury St Edmunds is the sugar beet capital of Europe. That's probably not true – some other lucky European city probably has that honour – but at this time of the year, it certainly feels as though it is. Journeys that usually take ten minutes, can last a lifetime if you're stuck behind some ancient tractor and trailer made roadworthy for the beet harvest.

If you manage to avoid the traffic queues, you'll probably skid in the quagmires of mud and boulders of fallen beet that turn the lanes into skating rinks. Every inhabitant of Bury should be allowed a free carwash, courtesy of British Sugar to sluice off the carapace of dirt that camouflages their cars from November till January.

Pity the poor locals, inhaling the Smell. The rest of the year it's a pleasant burnt caramel aroma that we inhale eight miles away, but this month the pall of rotting foliage from the lagoons hangs over the whole town. The factory site, surrounded by queues of vehicles delivering beet, looks from a distance, like a lunar landscape or the baddie's hideout in an early Bond movie – with chimneys belching steam and strange shaped hangars that house a world-destroying missile that will slowly rise from its centre.....

Heavily subsidised by the EU, and accused of depriving farmers in the developing world from livelihoods growing cane sugar, local agriculture round here depends on this unattractive crop, and for the moment there seems to be no fall in production. And it looks as though the view through the gate at the bottom of the garden next year will be of sugar beet.

2nd

The leaves are turning colour at last. Race to Charlotte's garden and pick trugfuls of *Quercus rubra*, London plane, and liquidambar; Virginia creeper, *Magnolia grandiflora* and tiny scarlet acers; and birch, beech and oak leaves and store them snugly between sheets of newspaper to dry flat under mats in every room in the house.

Discover a forgotten cache of bay leaves under the sitting room mat, and pop them in a jar in the kitchen. Then on to Wendy Smith's barn, where she sells floristry supplies, to collect the wire frames to make the wreaths for the shop and decorating course.

Loading the frames in the car, I notice a corner of the boot has a large hole, and next to it are tufts of insulation material, and next to that, horror of horrors, is a pile of droppings. Rat droppings!

I buy my chicken feed weekly from Mill Farm up at Pakenham where the Bryant family have been millers for generations. A timeless spot, on top of a hill, with the working windmill in the background, where one can buy feed for animals and birds, pick up bedding and gaze spellbound at a notice board covered with small ads. Do I want some jill ferrets, or a friendly Russell terrier, a pair of metal gates, a helping hand in the paddock, point of lay pullets? Not at the moment, but Mr. Bryant and I pass the

time of day and I go off with two sacks of mixed corn and a couple of bags of sunflower seeds in the boot.

Often, when I get home, I don't have the strength to lift the sacks of the corn out, so the car becomes a mobile feed hopper, and it seems – home to a rat. The thought of him hitching a ride perhaps, being blasted by my adolescent choice of blues, reggae, rock and pop through powerful speakers, chewing the electrics…….. Nip back to the Mill and Mr Bryant supplies a sachet, which soon disappears. There have been no further signs of life in the boot.

We all live within a few feet of a rat apparently. Here in the countryside, as the fields are harvested, rodents and other furry friends look for shelter in gardens and yards (and garages, it seems). It is a big problem. If you supply food as well, and chicken feed is ideal, they will set up home, breed, undermine the run and spread disease. It's this last trait that's the clincher. I quite like rats. Max used to keep one, called Roni Size (after a drum & bass DJ), and he was clever, friendly, though sadly, always rather smelly.

The hen keeper's armoury in the battle against vermin now includes organic poison, pasta based, and bait with poison that is rat specific, but whatever you choose should always be placed in a long drainpipe or covered with a cloche to keep your flock and other animals safe. Always react

267

straight away, don't wait, thinking they'll move on. They won't, and the milder winters no longer interrupt their breeding season.

3rd

Walnuts nearly dry. Pack them in nets of thirty, and label them. Hurray, we must have at least fifty bags for sale. At last, some pure profit. Celebrate with this wonderful pud:

Baked apple stuffed with caramelized walnut and ginger. Melt 2oz/60g sugar in a heavy pan till it turns golden. Pour in a little hot water. Take care, it will splatter. Stir till it turns syrupy. Mix in 4oz/125g of chopped or broken walnuts and a few finely sliced pieces of preserved ginger. Take four large Bramley apples and core. Fill the fruit with the mixture and cover with the sauce. Bake in a hot oven till apples are soft.

4th

Frosty morning in the garden, thankfully pull on my thermal gardening gloves. I notice most of the garden gurus on telly don't wear gloves. Always look after your hands. I never used to bother, but now wouldn't dream of going out with bare hands, whatever the weather. There is no excuse.

At the risk of sounding pushy, The Kitchen Garden stocks a great range of gloves, developed by the trawler fishing industry, but ideal for gardeners in any situation: light and aerated for hot weather offering lots of control for fiddly jobs, like weeding and dealing with seedlings; thornproof for pruning and general gardening; and warm and toasty for heavy work in the winter. But any gloves are better than cracked, infected skin and roughened, reddened hands.

I make a big bowl of Tapenade, to liven up the sort of snacks I eat as I work: a baked potato, a goat's cheese sandwich, tomato bruschetta, a plate of pasta, fast food to keep me going through this busy time.

Take a large jar of pitted black olives in brine and drain, rinsing thoroughly. Pop two chopped cloves of garlic, a tablespoonful of mustard and one of rinsed capers in a bowl and add half the olives. Blend and slacken using good olive oil. Add the rest of the jar of olives, the zest and juice of a lemon, a little salt and a few sprigs of thyme. Blend again. Tapenade will last for a week, covered in the fridge.

8th

No eggs today, almost for the first time this year. Traditionally, hens are supposed to lay between Valentine's Day and Guy Fawkes, (with broodies, mums and moulters taking short breaks). This year, my ladies have followed tradition almost to the day. But the coquettish new pullets, nearing 24 weeks of age, are what's known in the trade as point-of-lay.

Their little faces, comb and wattles are reddening so it won't be long before they surprise us with their first offering - occasionally the size of a blackbird's egg – nature being kind for a change. Best to pop a china egg in the nestbox, if there are no other layers to show them where to lay. I shall have to keep an eye on the Cockerel too, and make sure he isn't showing too much interest in them, keeping a couple of Orpington saddles to hand.

A lovely card from a couple who moved to France, taking with them some of our hatching eggs. The picture showed three Orpington hens sitting under a blue Citroen *Deux Chevaux* – successfully hatched from our stock, and now famous throughout the peasant farming community of the Limousin, for their impressive size, their magnificent plumage, their statuesque beauty. Proof at last that *les anglais* can do something right, and they haven't seen a cock yet.

11th

Through the window I can see the rotting pile of apples attracting wasps and peacock butterflies, blackbirds, thrushes, robins and moorhens. Not wasted after all. Today we posted 1300 invitations to our Christmas Shopping days. Fingers crossed for a good season.

12th

With my two new magazine columns of 700 and 900 words completed, smugly, I head off out to the cut flower garden to plant half the tulips. Two rows of 'Black Knight' (dark red), one of 'Apricot Beauty', and one of 'Princess Irene' (orange with green streaks) in one bed and then the same in the bed opposite. I hope I'll remember to plant the other half in a fortnight's time, and see if I get staggered flowering in the spring to get tulips flowering over a longer period. I find though, they usually catch up with one another, and still all appear in one gorgeous show.

A five minute interview on Radio Scotland, commenting on recent reports that commercial free range eggs are often mislabelled and not as free range as they seem. Would the

270

safest solution be to keep your own hens? I agreed, but naughtily omitted to mention mine weren't laying at all, yet.........

14th

Race into Bury along lanes littered with the squashed carcasses of 1000 pheasants, but the carnage of these poor birds on the roads is as nothing compared to the regular slaughter of the huge shoots. I realize farmers have to diversify, and that we owe much of our landscape to the shooting estates, but it's the scale of the massacres that perturbs me.

Collect jams from Mr Honeyball in Waitrose's car park. A magnificent range this year. And rush back with more deliveries to unpack, label and price. Every mass-produced product seems to need altering: a nasty label, less packaging, a new hanger, nothing is quite right and I put my stamp on everything.

Jean used to say the shop was a huge ego trip. The house looks like a demented Santa's grotto with boxes of goodies, piles of toys and products stacked everywhere. Thank heavens Keith comes tomorrow and I'll have somewhere to display all this stuff.

15th

Keith arrives to help turn Church Cottage into the Kitchen Garden department store. I know this will sound

disloyal to my husband, but as time went on, getting things repaired and mended was a difficult tightrope act. One had to choose the right moment to ask, offer services in return, and hang around helping. To be fair, originally Jean loved making and mending things – this house just wouldn't exist without his ingenuity and hard work, but eventually his loyalties were transferred to his boat and the house suffered.

What bliss it is now to write a list of what needs doing, to pay for it to be done (male pride denied this as an option in the past) and to have it done with enthusiasm. I'm guilt-ridden as I write this, but maybe others who live with sailors or golfers suffer similarly? So now, the wonderful Keith comes here once a month to do the jobs I just can't manage, and moving large pieces of furniture is one of them. The huge dresser is moved from the study, where it houses all my books, into the dining room which then turns into the kitchen department, and so on, till the transformation is complete.

We then live in a strange limbo, with our possessions in boxes for the next month, with nowhere to sit apart from our bedrooms, our lives taken over by the shop.

24th

Today I will plant out the 100 'White Pearl' hyacinth bulbs that Mary has grown in big boxes of bulb fibre, into the varied pots I've been collecting all year.

Luckily the weather is mild and dry. I wander over to the churchyard to pick up moss from the north side of the church, near the attractive Gothic portaloo, where the wind, or is it the birds, have dislodged it from the roof.

When the bulbs are snugly entered in their new containers, they get an eiderdown of moss, or sometimes a layer of gravel or coloured alpine screed, depending on my mood.

This time last year, just as the hens were putting themselves to bed, there was a sickening noise outside of birds screaming. Horrified, Jacques and I raced out to a garden covered in feathers, to see a woman ineffectually chasing a dog who was chasing a hen. Adrenalin pumped, we joined the chase, and eventually the dog was pulled off down the lane without apology, and we were left with one bird wounded and the rest traumatized. My friend a vet, was called. She patched and injected, but strangely the next day, the wounded bird had recovered, but one of the others had died of shock.

Most people manage to train their own pets to ignore their flock. Some take it to the other extreme, like my neighbour's Lhasa Apso – Pepsi, who shares duties with their mother hen, like some hairy *au pair*. But other people's dogs are another matter. The danger to poultry from foxes is well-trumpeted, but your hens' main predators are more likely to be uncontrolled dogs.

My friend and Orpington breeder, Pauline, was welcomed home the other day by her tearful daughter to the shocking news that her entire breeding flock, built up over years of selection, care and affection, had been slaughtered by two local dogs. Those that hadn't been torn to pieces, had been scared to death.

So, here's a plea to owners of dogs that stray, control your pets, but also to us as hen keepers to make good our boundaries and protect our birds. We are now the proud possessors of a pair of double gates to the drive that would grace the entrance to South Fork.

25th

Spend the weekend at the kitchen table, surrounded by dried seedheads, twigs, beads, wire and leaves retrieved from beneath every mat in the house, plus a few that have been stored between the pages of dusty, seldom-used cookery books. Tripping over wired wreath frames of every shape and size, I try to match colours with shapes to create attractive decorations to sell and embellish the shop.

I always start by attaching a fine copper wire loop to the frame of my choice so, if necessary, I can hang it up out of harm's way. Then I zigzag a layer of ribbon around the frame to give the leaves extra support. With trusty glue gun in hand, I stick them securely to the frame. I find the larger leaves look best on angled frames, but smaller ones suit flatter shapes, and look simply stunning hung in front of windows to catch the low winter sunlight.

Finish on Sunday afternoon, making two dozen cardoon nightlights. First I wind a piece of green florist's wire round the base of the stem and circle the flower head, returning and finishing off at the base. This is to stop the cardoon disintegrating later. Wearing fine gloves to protect my fingers from the prickles, I scoop out the choke with florists snips to form a small well and then insert a nightlight with a blob of glue. Typing this a few days later, my fingers are still sore.

Really tired, living on adrenalin, slightly manic, awake at night and up with a start and an endless list of things to do.

276

Not long to go now, the worst will be over and Jacques will be back soon.

27th

Everything has to be finished by today. Last deliveries: 10 beautiful paintings of hens and cocks by Kate and Hannah. Immediately see at least four I'd like to keep myself. This is hopeless. Jan appears with 55 puddings, 25 Christmas and 55 chocolate truffle cakes. Mick brings in trays of local honey and honeycomb from his hives across the fields. Barbara arrives with jars of her Seville marmalade, and walnut preserve. Max cleans the house with usual good grace, ready for the course tomorrow, while I price the last few items and fiddle.

28th

10.30 arrival of ten ladies for the Christmas Course. Advertised by the magazine as:

'A special one day course on how to create fabulous presents and decorations for your home, making use of natural materials. Start with homemade biscuits in Francine's kitchen, then a demonstration how to create seasonal displays using materials from the garden including seeds, and dried leaves, which can be used for wreaths, decorations and garlands. Penny Hands will demonstrate how to make a range of presents using garden produce, such as nuts, fruits and vegetables into liqueurs, preserves and desserts. Plus expert advice on packaging and presentation.

Match Pot with

Finally, you can enjoy tea and an exclusive preview of the Kitchen Garden store, before you leave with a goody bag.'

For lunch, we had Roast Tomato and Pepper Soup with Rena's Mediterranean bread, topped off with a piece of Jan's notorious chocolate truffle cake with mascarpone sprinkled with cinnamon. But during the afternoon we also tasted Penny's chutneys, truffles, biscuits, preserves, pickles, spiced nuts, clementines in vodka, sloe gin etcetera, etcetera, etcetera.

One homemade present that is always impressive is a jar of homemade preserved lemons.

First find a spectacular large wide-mouthed jar, then buy enough unwaxed lemons to fill it. Score their well-washed skins lengthways and pack the cuts with cooking salt. Pack them tightly into your jar and top up with brine (1oz/25g salt to 1pt/600ml boiled, cooled water). Add a few fresh bay leaves, then a thin layer of cooking oil to seal. Close the lid tightly. Un-opened, these lemons will keep for at least a year and are useful for cooking, especially in North African dishes.

30th

First egg from the new girlies. Beige tinted, regular sized and welcome. Mrs L's Luncheon for 15. This is a Kitchen Garden tradition. For ten years this nice lady has thrown a party here for her friends and they have launched our season. They have always been brilliant customers and I'm very grateful for their patronage, but it's a tight squeeze, serving lunch amid all the stock.

The menu this year:
Roast Tomato and Red Pepper Soup (again).

Roast a big pan of tomatoes and a big pan of deseeded red peppers in a hot oven with a few cloves of garlic, sea salt and black pepper. When cooked, fry four red onions with a teaspoon of Ras-el-hanout, or mixed spices on the stove in a large pan.

When soft add the roasted peppers and tomatoes, a carton of tomato pureé and 2pts/1.2l of Marigold, sluicing out the roasting pans with stock. Mix well and pass through a mouli or fine metal sieve. (A fiddly task, one that I've spent my last two evenings pursuing.) Serve with crème fraîche and plenty of chopped broad leaf parsley.

Served with Rena's Mediterranean Bread that will turn a bowl of soup into a meal.

This is a scone recipe that substitutes olive oil for fat. Mix together 6oz/175g self raising flower, 2 tablespoon each of oil and milk, a teaspoon of baking powder and a large egg. Flavour with a tiny amount of mustard powder and cayenne to taste. Add chopped sundried tomatoes and pine nuts or pickled walnuts or olives and top with a little strong cheese – feta, pecorino or parmesan.

Penny's Lemon Polenta Cake, adapted from the River Café Cookbook.

Heat the oven to 160C/325F and butter a 9in/24cm springform cake tin, lining the base with baking parchment. Beat 8oz/250g butter till soft and

281

pour in 8oz/250g caster sugar and beat again. Stir in 8oz/250g ground almonds, 1 teaspoon vanilla extract, and then 3 beaten eggs, one at a time, beating as you go. Fold in the zest of 2 lemons, and the juice of another, 4oz/125g instant medium polenta, 1 teaspoon baking powder and a good pinch of salt.

Spoon the mixture into the prepared tin, and bake till a golden brown – about 50 minutes, Penny finds is just right. Test by piercing the middle with a skewer, it should come out clean. Dust with icing sugar. This is a beautiful cake and will show off your hens' yellow yolks perfectly. We decorated this as a pudding with a few blueberries.

As the ladies leave laden with shopping after their lunch, the shop then previews with a glass of damson gin, to friends till eight. Now that the stock is displayed and priced and the hard work is done, I enjoy being a shopkeeper, pointing out new products and chatting. Many customers complain that they buy bags of goodies for themselves and seem to forget all about their present list.

Discuss the bird flu problem with Tom, a poultry breeder, while his wife shops. It seems the Autumn migration is almost complete without further cases in Europe. Of course, the disease rumbles on with dire consequences and loss of life in the Far East and Africa, which is where they say the next threat will come from, with birds migrating in springtime.

Email from Jacques, they are packing. I can't wait. Exhausted, I fall into bed.

286

DEC*ember*

Decorations

Homecomings

Christmas Shopping

Celebrations

Roast Goose

All the Trimmings

Champagne Sorbet

1st

I barely notice it's winter in the run up to December. Darkness draws in early, but I'm working hard with lots to look forward to. The unseasonably warm weather tricks people into thinking there are still many shopping days till Christmas. Difficult to decide when to start trading, how long to keep going and how best to maximize income in what is, after all, the only really profitable season in the shopkeepers' year.

I've always liked the fact my shop opens for just 10 days. Like a glorified jumble sale, the bargains go first, and once they've gone, that's it. The Kitchen Garden is a bizarre Aladdin's cave, a mixture of artefacts made especially for us – showcasing one offs by special makers and artists, some products I've customized, a little mass produced tat that's amusing or useful, a few antiques, and some old favourites.

Because it's Christmas, I concentrate on food. In the kitchen department (aka dining room), sit baskets of traditional cakes and puds from the redoubtable Jan at the Pantry, whose recipes have persuaded lifetime cooks to forgo cooking their own. Sweet things from Germany, France and Italy, all of whom seem to have more exciting traditions than ours: mouthwatering soft amaretti, to be eaten at the end of a meal with a glass of something festive; spiced gingerbread, and pretty marzipan and crystallized fruits.

Of course we sell locally produced delicacies: handmade truffles and sophisticated citrus peel dipped in dark chocolate and prunes steeped in brandy. (All enthusiastically finished off by me, if unsuccessful in tempting customers). For those with savoury tastes: champagne and raspberry vinegars, relishes, chutneys, pickles, sauces plus the usual fantastic range of jams and jellies from Mrs Honeyball, despite this year suffering the handicap of a broken arm (Mr Honeyball leapt into the breach – under instruction).

In the garden department (the conservatory) we sell tools, seeds, and eco-friendly products to feed and house wild birds. This section doubles up as the poultry department, with a wide range of practical and decorative hen-themed odd and ends – tasteful objects are difficult to source in this sphere.

The toy department is in the sitting room along with hand knitted woollies, alpaca cosy things from Scotland, handmade soaps from Norfolk, and candles, indoor sparklers and decorations. The shop outside is turned into a seasonal nursery stacked with baskets of cyclamen, glass jars of narcissi, pots of kitchen herbs, antique containers full of hyacinths and amaryllis, tabletop trees, and hellebores - the Christmas Rose.

The first two days are the busiest. Barbara helps at the cash desk, with Max packing, and taking purchases to cars, but during the following week I manage alone. Shoppers appear at a brisk pace, nice to natter, but I mustn't distract them from what, after all, is a bit of a chore.

Certainly I would hate to be going round the shops in town, where every retailer sells the same stock and parking is a

nightmare. Much better to struggle out to the sticks, wade through the mud and wander round an odd small department store in someone's house. Strange, how, after a while, the most outrageous ideas become the norm and one no longer sees the ridiculousness of a situation. But sometimes I do see a look of incredulity pass over the faces of newcomers as they wander in.

11th

So it's all over now for another year. I do my sums. A good year, less customers but overall they spent more. The leftover stock has all been packed away. Thank you Sainsbury's for your useful green stacking banana boxes, and Keith and Max have returned the furniture to its rightful place. The house looks sparse and empty, and there's work to be done in the chicken run.

Neglected, because the shop has taken up all my daylight hours, the hens are nonetheless looking rather smart. Their prolonged moult finally over, and with saddles briefly discarded until the Cockerel feels the sap rising yet again, the girls look stunning all together, with their glowing apricot feathers replacing the sunshine.

I scour out their houses, and notice the Cockerel has forsaken his summer quarters al fresco under the henhouse and moved into the shelter of the big house, usually the sole prerogative of the tiny black bantam. All the other ladies are in the main house, with the pullets still cramped in their

293

broody house. Now they've started laying, the Cockerel will soon lure them into his domain.

I move the strawbales on the verandah and find a hidden family of rats, dead and decaying, poisoned. A result, I suppose, but still sad to see the babes cuddled up to their mum. Mustn't be sentimental. As they say round here, the only good rat is a dead'un.

Clear the run, sweep the leaves and refill the dustbath with ashes from the woodburner. It takes an hour or two before the hens realize their luck, and then they're in, writhing in an ecstasy of feathery delight, scratching and fluffing, scraping and shaking, covering the run with a veil of grey ash until dusk, when it's a hearty supper of mixed corn that'll sustain them through the cold night, snug in their comfy clean roosts till dawn.

13th

Jean's birthday. He would have been 64 years old. Friends always said he would have made a mutinous old man, railing against the indignities of ageing, but the last thing anyone thought was that he wouldn't make old age at all. All his multitudinous family in Quebec survived well into their nineties. Best to concentrate on Max, his birthday falls a week later. I buy him a second hand welding machine. It is intensely satisfying and consoling to me that he has inherited his dad's practical abilities. And Jacques and Saskia, they'll be back on the 17th.

17th

Homecoming. Two exhausted brown travellers, back to a huge welcome from both families and loads of friends. It's going to be a great Christmas.

18th

Woke this morning feeling fuzzier than last night's celebrations should justify, and realize the vision in one of my eyes is veiled and obliterated by Rorschach-like pen and ink drawings floating between me and the object in sight. This rings a bell and sends me fumbling in my diary for an old note from my doctor on vitreous separation – his diagnosis for a previous visual problem that resulted in flashing lights on the peripheries of my vision.

An hour or so later, I'm in the corridor at the Eye Clinic, watching the nurses wearing silly festive hats, complete with ink blot accessories. My pupils are dilated hugely by drops, and I'm waiting for the specialist, then staring into lights and being told there is a tear in my retina that must be repaired. So, I'm moved to another room and a lens is pressed against my anaesthetized eyeball and a laser beamed on to the retina to cause scarring that will fill and repair the tear. Although – as promised – it doesn't hurt, my whole being screams to protect my eye and close it, which of course, I can't.

Taxis later, I'm home with other appointments on my card, the promise that the floaters will disappear with time, and instructions not to exercise or drive at night. Later, in the small hours I'm terrified. Am I going blind? Those who are used to being part of a couple find that if good experiences aren't shared they don't exist, and bad things fester. I don't want to worry the kids.

22nd

Concentrate on decorating the house. As the year fades and autumn's shades have long since turned to the subtler tones of winter, I ransack the garden for one last time this year. There are still a few coloured leaves under the sitting room mat, flattened by customers' feet over the last fortnight and drying seed heads in the spare bedroom.

I place one of my favourite wreaths from this year's stock above the mantle piece – a collection of dried fig leaves with little stalks like delicate mouse tails. Though robust as living leaves, they dry friable, too brittle to sell, but are safe here, out of harm's way.

Picked at various stages in their degeneration, as they turned from green to yellow, to ochre and then brown. I cheated and added one more shade - burnished copper with a burst of aerosol paint. The other decoration I felt merited a 'not for sale' sticker was a simple flat wreath of glycerined single copper beech leaves, each centered with a slightly different coloured Smoke Tree *Cotinus coggygria* leaf. I thought it had a fashionable Seventies feel.

Using some lovely wire from Wendy's with loops at either end, I string together my garden bounty: well-spaced small bunches of honesty seedheads, old man's beard, quaking grass, single orange physalis lanterns and Miss Wilmott's ghostly dried eringiums. It looks sparsely effective. That will have to do. It's hard to focus.

23rd
My sons think happiness is a full fridge. They still walk

straight up to it each time they enter the house and open the door, the fridge light shedding its beneficent beam, as though it's all there is between them and starvation, even when they don't live here.

I love a full larder and all the Christmas extras: the medlar jelly to go with the goose; Barbara's Walnut Relish, made with her own trees' nuts, chopped apples, dates and this year with walnut vinegar, enhancing the cheese course; the Italian mince pie filling with figs and pine nuts; and a long list of goodies that Penny Hands and I showcased in our book, A Christmas Journal, "...with delicious seasonal recipes, bright ideas for presents, plus space to add your own special celebrations – ingredients that make this journal a reminder of good times spent in the company of loved ones. Recipes from the Kitchen Garden's larder will add to your traditional fare and offer a safe place to keep cuttings and recipes, lists and addresses with family souvenirs and suggestions." So says the blurb on the cover.

I put aside one day in the run up to the 25th to cook all the dishes that can be made in advance, so as to enjoy the important days without constantly disappearing to cook. The kitchen, dining room and sitting room all merge into one another here, so it's impossible to disappear, but it's hard to concentrate, cooking in company.

First, I make the spiced red cabbage dish that we traditionally eat with the goose and the aroma of juniper takes me back to Christmas past. Those with family members missing, for what ever reason, are forgiven a little sentimentality at this time. Sometimes memories are hard to bear. Jean loved celebrating, adored feast days and messing about in the kitchen and we miss him. I take solace in preparing these familiar dishes:

Planted in early summer, our red cabbage has spent the growing season in a cage, to prevent the ravages of the cabbage white. Chopping the cabbage as finely as possible, I fry a couple of red onions and green apples in a little olive oil with a tablespoon of light muscovado sugar. I pound garlic, sea salt, juniper berries and coloured peppercorns with a pestle and sprinkle them into the pan together with ground allspice, a clove or two and then the shredded cabbage. Cooked for 15 minutes with a splash of balsamic vinegar and the lid tight on, this vibrant spicy dish goes perfectly with roast goose, hot or cold.

Root vegetables are the season's staple crop and often considered the kitchen garden's poor relations. The French dismiss them as fodder for beasts, but treated with respect and plenty of butter, goose fat and seasonal herbs, this dish of comforting, creamy mash comes as a textural relief to all the crispy bits that make up the Christmas meal. Most can be left underground to over-winter in the vegetable garden's soil till needed.

Dig up a few boulder-like celeriac 'Monarch', some giant parsnips, a handful of knobbly Jerusalem artichokes tubers ('Fuseau' is the least knobbly) and a couple of sweet potatoes (Thompson & Morgan T65 slips crop successfully, even in this climate).

Peel these vegetables as best you can, and cube. Collect and clean a few leeks and slice finely. Fry some cumin in a little goosefat or butter, adding all the vegetables and fry till sealed. Ladle in enough Marigold stock to stop the contents sticking. Cover and turn the heat low. When tender, mash with a spoonful or two of crème fraîche and season with grated nutmeg, salt and black pepper. This is a rough mash and not a smooth puree. Store in a shallow dish, so it will heat up quickly, dotted with butter and grated nutmeg when needed.

Although I love Christmas pud, I think Christmas day is possibly the worst time to eat it. Replete and happy after the main course, I believe this Champagne Sorbet from Penny Hands is a lighter and more elegant alternative.

1pt/600ml champagne or sparkling wine
¼ pt/150ml syrup
(made with 4oz/125g sugar dissolved in ¼ pt/150ml boiling water cooled.)
1 wine glass brandy
Juice half lemon
1 lightly beaten egg white – frothy, but not stiff

Stir all the ingredients together in a large bowl and freeze according to the instructions given with your ice cream maker. Transfer in a plastic container into the freezer for at least 24 hours. Because of the high (be warned) alcohol content this sorbet never sets very hard, so can be served straight from the freezer, so you won't be struggling on the day. Scoop servings carefully into delicate champagne flutes.

24th

Christmas Eve is the most magical day of the holiday, the Europeans have got it right. Newly married, we spent Christmas in snowy Montreal with my husband's family, following old French traditions. *Les parents* went to midnight mass while we got drunk on Southern Comfort waiting to eat baked fish very late, round a candle-lit tree. It was fabulous, but Christmas

day itself was a non event. Tired and hungover, we stared at each other grumpily, played cards and fiddled desultorily with our presents.

This generation of *les Raymonds* often celebrates with a party. This year to welcome the travellers back, a dozen or so guests, of varying ages, the young moving on to party after eating. The table is decorated with a big wreath tied with bunches of perennial herbs, bay, rosemary, grey sage, orange and lemon thyme, garlic chive seedheads, and four fat candles, to be lit as the guests arrive.

Next to large dishes of spiced nuts to nibble, drenched with a coating of walnut oil and sprinkled with dark muscovado sugar, garam masala and sea salt, with a large pinch of cayenne pepper, roasted in the oven 180C/350F till golden brown.

We start the meal with a couple of Vacherin Mont D'Or cheeses melted in their wooden boxes with big platters of vegetable chips to dip in.

Chop celeriac, sweet potatoes, parsnips and Jerusalem artichokes into chunky chips and pat dry. Place on a baking tray, covered with oiled, greaseproof paper and brush with a little spicy Morrocan harissa paste diluted with olive oil. Sprinkle with sea salt and sesame seeds and pop onto the top shelf of a hot oven until nicely browned. Serve piping hot, ready to dip into the Vacherin (or Brie or Camembert)

in its own wooden box melted for five minutes in a medium oven until runny.

A rich pungent aroma comes from the big black French lidded cast iron pan (that cost more than three times I paid for my first car) bought from the Elizabeth David shop, and we lift the lid to a spicy vibrant orange butternut squash, apple and pear soup.

Fry some garlic, an onion, a Bramley apple, two Conference pears and a peeled, chopped squash in a knob of butter and a little olive oil till soft. Add two cloves, a cinnamon stick and a bayleaf, or a teaspoon of Ras-el-Hanout – an exotic Moroccan spice and herb blend of rosebuds, nigella, lavender, cassia plus the usual suspects - and pour in 1½ pints/850 ml of stock and a glass of white wine. Process in a blender and stir in a tub of single cream. Serve sprinkled with sage leaves fried to a crisp in butter (a fragrant topping that pairs just as well with a plate of steaming pasta asciutta).

The soup is served with a huge slab of focaccia topped with red peppers and black olives. As a child we were always sent a box of apricots from relations in South Africa so they have been a family Christmas tradition ever since.

For pudding we eat a large dish of apricots stuffed with homemade walnut and almond marzipan, baked in the oven with a little orange water and served with mascarpone sprinkled with cinnamon.

305

25th

Christmas may not be a moveable feast, but family circumstances change, especially as offspring leave home, and the focus on celebrations shift. This has been our *modus operandii* for the last few years. Since sadly, there is no longer an excited rush to open stockings in the morning, brunch is at midday and the menu consists of what we would have had as our first course at the main meal, this year a tasty fishy mixed smoked platter from the Borley Smokery (from our local farmers' market) served with rye bread and horseradish relish.

Then we open our small collection of presents, and gradually get round to dealing with the goose. Champagne flows. People help and come and go, and the whole day revolves around the preparation and eating of the meal without deadlines or timetables. Spicy smells fill the whole house and stimulate our appetites for 5-ish, when roast goose with red cabbage and juniper, vegetable mash and Max's amazing potatoes roasted in goose fat appear on the table, with all the trimmings.

I'll pause here, contradict myself and give an exact timetable to cook goose. It is a delicious meat, often disregarded because of its fatty reputation. It would be a tragedy for anyone to return to turkey without once trying using this method we've tested over twenty five years:

It's worth remembering a) that goose meat needs to be cooked for 20 minutes per pound, so a 10lb goose will take about 3½ hrs; b) that it is a long bird and will often only fit in the oven diagonally across the pan; and c) that turning a goose spitting with hot fat is not a job for one pair of hands, so don't send all the family out for a walk.

Start: *place goose, stuffed with quartered apples and onions, seasoned with ground juniper and rubbed with sea salt, upside down on a trivet in a deep pan in a pre-heated oven at 375F/190C.*

½ hr later, *pull out the pan and carefully prick all over with a skewer to allow the fat to escape.*

After an hour, pour off the fat into a large jam jar (containing a metal spoon so the glass doesn't crack.) Reduce the heat to 350F/180C.

1hr later: *Pour off fat again. Turn right side up and baste.*

1hr later: *Cover with foil and place in warm bottom oven till you're ready to eat.*

Out into the chilly garden just before the light falls, searching for a sprig of parsley. The only herb I can find in the desolate wastes of the veg plot is chervil, to sprinkle on the mash. Back into the smokey goosefat atmosphere, Jacques and Max are playing chess, their heads together over the board, drinking cans of lager, listening to White Stripes on my new ipod (their present to me, ready loaded with my own adolescent selection of chosen tunes), the mood testosterone-charged, then as the goose rests, civilization returns, a glass of Brown Brothers' sparkling Pinot Meunier and the feast begins.

Various puddings, cheese with pickled quinces, nuts and chocolates are picked at throughout the evening between games, the odd decent television programme, phone calls to absent family and more music.

I have kept diaries of Christmases past, ranging from 1978, the year our eldest was born and I noted we had English wine with our gravadlax,

Pommard with our goose, Sauternes with our pud and possets on our smart clothes probably; to the year both boys were travelling and Jean and I had a massive feast to ward off the freezing cold on his boat; to Dickensian gatherings of extended family. We try to always buy local food, but add a touch of the exotic as well. It is Christmas after all. A change of menu can be exhilarating, but be prepared for alterations to the norm to be greeted with suspicion from your children. I find they are the fiercest upholders of family traditions.

28th

In the vacuous and rather depressing no-man's land between Christmas and New Year, watching too much television. The cat on my lap watches too. I can see her ears prick up. She and I are particularly fond of wildlife programmes, but our opinions diverge on the subject of Bill Oddie.

Rummaging through the larder, I come across various bottles of home-made alcohol. Just the right moment to sample the raspberry vodka bottled in September. Not bad, but needs a little more sugar, though not as tasty as the Quince ratafia vintage 2004, but the outright winner is the Damson Gin we bottled in October – a rich smooth ruby tincture, belying its cheap gin origins. Vodka is probably the best value for home bottling, gin is good but brandy is better. Sloes, morello cherries, kumquats and prunes are all good preserved in booze. Other more exotic combinations of fruit and liquor start to swim past my eyes. Enough, perhaps.

Time to take stock. Not an easy year. Apart from the staggeringly worrying global situation, on both ecological and religious fronts, which are somehow too overwhelming to grapple with, personally it has been a challenging time. Starting, pathetically in comparison, with the loss of my painstakingly compiled mailing lists and friendships involved; the misleading advice and consequent expensive mistakes made during the setting up of the Henkeepers' Association; and nervous tracking of a travelling son, all are outweighed by the bird flu tragedy causing the culling of millions of creatures, destruction of livelihoods and threatening far worse – small consequence my declining book sales.

As my generation ages, special friends suffer worrying illnesses, some don't survive them sadly, and one's own pathetic health problems are easily magnified – proved latterly with unfounded worries about my eye, now on the mend, the floating veil lifting slowly. All these problems sap confidence and cause pain, especially when largely dealt with alone.

But I've been lucky, looking back: the Henkeepers' Association has well over a thousand members – admittedly just a small proportion of the reputed ½ million backyard poultry owners, but compared with Poultry Club membership after 150 years, it's a good start. We have a voice at Defra, though who knows whether it is listened to, and hopefully when more easily-administered vaccines are available they will join the existing cocktail that is currently injected into poultry. We need to pray for deliverance from

311

the virus till then. Business has improved, book sales are increasing, I write two regular, monthly magazine columns, (a little financial stability at last) and have high hopes for this diary. Hopes are as necessary as realities. And it's lovely to have Jacques and Saskia back.

More than anything I value my friends, my family, my boys. Their love and support is my most important asset, but strangely, so is my independence. I adore this place, this small domestic landscape, my tiny kingdom, but if I had to abandon it for any reason, especially to enable my sons an easier start in life, I would. The future, on a good day, holds no particular fears. This, after all, is all there is.

Let's drink one last glass to the closing year, the most important toast of all – Your Health - Santé!

Clearspring Miso	www.clearspring.co.uk
Dragonfly Teas	www.dragonflyteas.com
Spice Mixes	www.seasonedpioneers.co.uk
Bamix Mixers	www.scottsofstow.co.uk
Marigold Stock	www.marigoldhealthfoods.com
Rare Breeds Society	01934 833 619
Seeds of Italy	www.seedsofitaly.com
Suffolk Herbs	www.suffolkherbs.com
Borley Smokery	01787 373 174
Defra	www.defra.gov.uk
Call Duck Club	www.callducks.net
Garden Station	www.thegardenstation.co.uk
Assington Mill	www.assingtonmill.com
Practical Poultry Magazine	www.practicalpoultry.com
Smallholder Magazine	www.smallholder.co.uk
The English Garden Magazine	www.theenglishgarden.co.uk
Martins Nursery	01449 737 698
Wyken Hall Farmers Market	www.wykenvineyards.co.uk
Kate & Hannah Breach	01953 483 380

Essex Gardens' Trust	www.gardenstrust.org.uk
Humanist Society	www.humanism.org.uk
Elm Farm Research Centre	www.efrc.com
The Soil Association	www.soilassociation.org
Clare Bulb Company	www.clare-bulbs.co.uk
Samphire	www.samphireshop.co.uk
Museum of Garden History	www.museumofgardenhistory.org
Omlet Henhouses	www.omlet.co.uk
Dubarry Boots	www.dubarryboots.com
W & M Smith	www.florists-supplies.co.uk
Bryants Mill Farm Feeds	01359 230 277
The Poultry Club of Great Britain	www.poultryclub.org
Marshalls Seeds	www.marshalls-seeds.co.uk

The Kitchen Garden is open on Fridays & Saturdays (10 – 5) from Easter till the end of September, and during the first week of December for Christmas. For information and to view our catalogue and book list, visit our website – www.kitchen-garden-hens.co.uk

Join the Henkeepers' Association for free online up-to-date poultry information and register your support for AI vaccination: www.henkeepersassociation .co.uk.

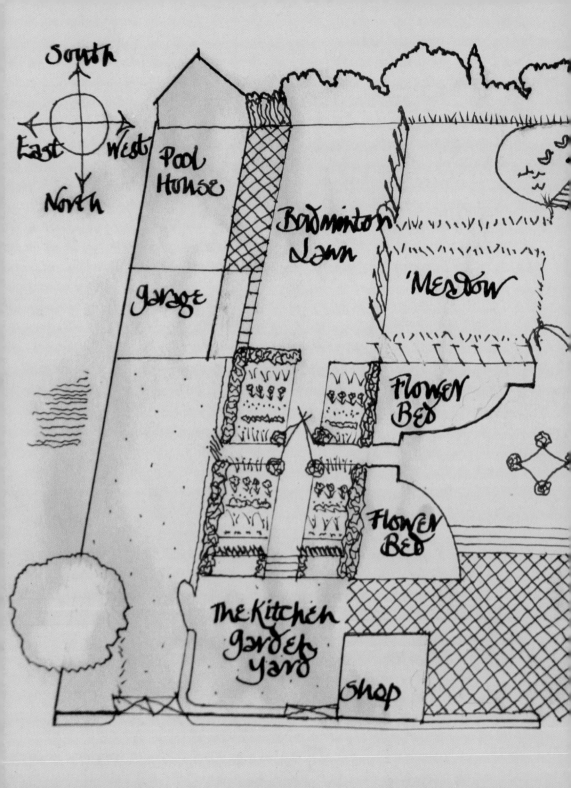